LIFE LEAVES CLUES™

reach your ultimate potential... clue by clue

by Bryan Thayer

Thayer, Bryan
    Life Leaves Clues - Reach Your Ultimate Potential… Clue by Clue
ISBN 978-0-9672098-2-1
    1. Business 2. Self Help

Printed in the United States of America

ENDORSEMENTS

"You'll discover hidden treasures that were right under your nose."
SUCCESS magazine

"I laughed, smiled, cried, and left the book determined to be a better man, husband, and father. Your personal stories are so real and relevant. The behind-the-scenes info you provided to set up stories about other inspiring people made each moment intriguing. The Wind It Up sections at the end of each chapter gave me concrete actions to take. Congratulations!"
—Dave Blanchard CEO, The Og Mandino Group
Author, *Today I Begin a New Life* and *The Observer's Chair*

"Most people get so caught up in busy-ness of life they forget to focus, to quietly observe what's happening around them and what they can learn from it. This book shows you how to see, get clarity, and interpret those valuable experiences. Well done, Bryan!"
—Tony Jeary, The RESULTS Guy™

"Success is predictable if you know what determines it. If you want to strengthen your life and your effectiveness, you'll discover a great friend in this book. You'll recommend it to all your friends."
—Jim Britt, Author, *Rings of Truth*

"A transformative book unlike any before it."
—Andrew Tanner, Author, Speaker

ACKNOWLEDGMENTS

It isn't possible to thank all those who have shared so many wonderful clues with me—at least, not without writing an entire book of appreciations. But please allow me to acknowledge the kindness of those who have given of their time and talent to *Life Leaves Clues*.

To all of my children and my amazing wife, Jackie, thank you for your love, support, and constant encouragement.

Thank you, Don Ward, Richard Brooke, Denise Earl, Lisa May, Sean Murphy, Jackie and David Lindsey, Drew Earl, Alan Peterson, Brittney Gillespie, Rick and Lisa Evenson, Guy Lindsey, Ed Griffin, Kellene Adams, Rod Clifford, and Michael Boyd for your brilliant feedback and insights.

Creative direction and design came together with the artistic talents of Michael Hancock and Bryan Moore. Thank you for your skilled art direction.

Finally, a special thanks to my editor, Sara Wigington. I am grateful to have such a dear friend to work with on this project—one who literally can finish my sentences. You are like a sister to me. It has been a complete joy working with a gifted writer who is as passionate about sharing life's clues as I am.

CONTENTS

FOREWORD

You know how some people just collect things? Baseball cards, porcelain dolls, rare coins, stamps, spoons.

Not me. For most of my life, I've been collecting clues. Life clues. The kind of clues that make you go, "Hmmm."

I do it because I'm constantly amazed by the people around me and the things I see and hear that just make sense. More clues exist than any one person could uncover in a lifetime.

Much of this book was written on napkins, in the margins of good books, on my phone's notes app. Any time I see or feel something that can make my life better, I write it down.

The fact is, this stuff is not new. It's been around as long as the human race has. "History doesn't repeat itself," Mark Twain said, "but it does rhyme." What's happening now rhymes with things that have already happened—things that have *been* happening. The clues in our lives will keep showing up like pieces of a puzzle until we finally pay attention, put them together, and make sense of them.

What I've come to know is, those who live extraordinary lives have learned to pay attention to the clues life leaves them. They see, hear, and feel at above-average levels. It's almost like they can see around corners, take mental notes on what the world is teaching them, and still pay attention to the road directly ahead.

This book is a collection of some of the most critical clues I've found and learned to follow. It's no accident you're holding it in your hands right now. Finding your clues and following where they lead you can put you on the right path for becoming who you are meant to be.

INTRODUCTION

Every day, whether you realize it or not, you look for clues. You need them to get along in life. Some clues are subtle, like the social clues you watch for to determine if someone is really interested in what you're saying. Others are more obvious and easy to find, like when you check the gas gauge in your car or when you check your weather app before you decide what to wear.

Clues are in the things you see, the words you hear, and the people you meet, and you constantly use them to solve the mysteries of your own life. They can tell you when to keep going, when to slow down, even when to stop. This book is all about those clues. I'm going to uncover some of them and make it easier for you to see and act on the clues life leaves for you.

The way we use the word *clue* today evolved from a story about finding one's way. In a famous myth, a Greek hero named Theseus battled the Minotaur, a half-man, half-bull monster that lived in a labyrinth on the island of Crete. After slaying the Minotaur, Theseus faced yet another challenge: he had to find his way out of the intricate maze. But he had thought ahead. He had unraveled a ball of string to leave a trail as he entered, so finding his way out was as easy as rolling up the string again.

In the English language, the word *clew* originally meant a globe or ball made by winding up string or yarn. In about the fourteenth century, *clew* (now *clue*) got an entirely new twist. Because of the story of Theseus, it came to mean using hints and tips to figure out a mystery.

When you refine the skill of rolling up your ball of string—following your instincts, paying attention to the clues in your life—you will find yourself happier and more productive than ever, and you'll become more confident that you're on the right track.

Did you ever realize that a good movie is all about giving you one clue after another as the plot unfolds? Many movies are based on the thrilling idea that following obscure clues can lead you to hidden secrets or riches. The *Indiana Jones* series starring Harrison Ford is a good example. After searching old books and archives, Dr. Jones, a college professor of antiquities, would venture out with clues or an old, arcane map to find an article of great historic value.

You may have seen *National Treasure*, where actor Nicholas Cage portrays a modern-day Indiana Jones. He is seeking an incredible treasure hidden in the capitol of the greatest country on earth. The most important clue was hidden in the most obvious of places, the heavily guarded Declaration of Independence. Fictional adventures like these are the key ingredients for stories and entertainment. There is a reality here, however. Clues to success and happiness are all around us. They are hidden in plain view, available to anyone who is willing to look for them.

Some clues can change a person or a family. Some can change much more than that. One particular clue, written hundreds of years ago in the margin of a book and then pondered upon, altered the destiny of mankind and even your place in the western hemisphere—yes, you personally.

If you've ever been swimming with friends, you've probably played Marco Polo. To play, one person closes his eyes and calls, "Marco!" while everyone else replies, "Polo!" The blinded player judges by the direction of the voices where the other players are and tries to tag them. The game gets its name from one of the greatest explorers of all time, the actual Marco Polo.

Polo was born in the year 1254. As a teenager, he traveled from Europe to Asia with his father and uncle. This was no small task 750 years ago. They crossed foreign lands and mountain ranges to distant and mysterious societies. Marco Polo returned to Italy after 24 years to find Venice at war with Genoa. He served on a galleon and was captured as a prisoner of war and incarcerated for one year.

While in prison, he dictated his memoirs to another prisoner, a writer named Rustichello da Pisa. The memoirs became the book known as (loosely translated) *The Travels of Ser Marco Polo*.

A couple hundred years after Marco Polo wrote his book, Christopher Columbus read it. Like Polo, Columbus was a sailor and adventurer. He ardently studied maps and the work of other writers and explorers. He studied the sea, sailing, cartography, and ships. By the time he was 30, he had chosen to be an ocean explorer. Ocean discovery up to that time had been southward, toward Africa. Few had dared to go west, where sea monsters and an endless waterfall awaited.

Columbus was about 40 when he was studying in the Columbian Library in Seville, Spain, and picked up the book by Marco Polo. There he found a clue so profound that he made a handwritten note in its margin. His note highlights Marco's observation that distant lands *were washed on the East by a great sea*.

Columbus may have imagined himself standing on the eastern shore of that distant land, facing Spain. He probably couldn't have known that what would become known as the Americas lay between, but as he pondered on that comment by Marco Polo, he must have realized that if Japan had a sea to the east, and Europe had a sea on the west, there was no endless waterfall. There was land. The earth must be round.

For some 3,000 years of recorded sailing history, no one had journeyed past Portugal except for the Vikings, who had ventured as far as what is now Nova Scotia almost 500 years earlier. But this clue set Columbus's mind to believe that he could travel west, which he did in October 1492. His courageous decision pierced the curtain, and fleets of explorers followed. The next 50 years saw more than a dozen countries launching hundreds of ventures into the new world, exploring both North and South America, where today we play Marco Polo in our pools.

Life is packed with clues. History is loaded with ideas that make sense and can lead us to success. Becoming what you should be is about finding your right path, following what you love, learning to work with your life, and doing what's right for you even if others can't see it.

I believe that life is your advocate, a team member that shows you clues made specifically for you that lead you to your ultimate potential. I hope you're ready to find it.

CHAPTER 1

THE LAW OF GRAVITY

The more you think about, work on, focus on, and ponder the things you want, the faster they will come to you. It's called the law of gravity, and it works the same way in the mind as it does with the earth and all the other planets. As mass increases, gravitational force increases. As mass decreases, gravitational force decreases. We all revolve around the biggest thing, the sun. It has the strongest pull and, lucky for us, the most light and warmth.

In your mind, you create gravity. Whatever you focus on becomes the biggest. It takes up the most space in your consciousness, and its gravitational force increases. Everything you think will revolve around this single focus.

What you think about, you bring about.

If you need a new dishwasher, for example, all of a sudden you will start seeing ads for dishwashers. They're everywhere. They've actually been there all along, but now that getting a dishwasher is on your mind, you take notice. Same with creating a business plan, losing weight, attracting new customers—anything that's important to you. Once you identify it as a real priority in your life, you'll start to see it more and more often.

The bigger the thing you're thinking about is, the more gravity it has, and the faster it comes to you. It's literally coming to you because both sides (you and that thing you want) are working. Those dishwasher ads were out there the whole time. They were in mailers, on billboards, and on television. But until you needed that dishwasher and started thinking about it every day, you didn't really notice. Now, with all those ads out there, and your need for that dishwasher, you and the dishwasher are going to come together. When both sides pull, the outcome happens more quickly.

Be careful. Gravity is powerful, and what you're afraid of also has a gravitational pull. Remember, we become what we focus on. If you live your life trying to avoid a situation you don't want, always thinking, *What if, what if, what if…* that what-if will find its way to you because it's taking up so much room in your heart and mind.

So here's what you do when you find yourself focusing on something negative or something that you're afraid of. Replace it with something positive you *do* want. This takes mental effort and practice. You might have to remind yourself 10 times an hour at first. But once you make the vision of what you want bigger than what you don't want, you're on your way.

My sons play baseball. I tell them that if they're nervous to strike out (who isn't, right?) and they focus on that what-if, they're actually more likely to strike out. But if they can visualize themselves connecting with the ball, getting a hit, running the bases, hearing the fans cheer, and high-fiving their teammates, they're way more likely to succeed. Does that visualization guarantee a base hit? No. But they're *more* likely to get that hit if that's what they focus on. On the other hand, they're very unlikely to get a hit if all they think about is striking out.

When you think about something and truly focus on it, you feed the gravitational pull of your mind. You act on what you think about, so be sure you think about what you really want! Make the vision of what you want bigger than the vision of what you don't want.

Visualize the end result.

Back in the 1460s a sculptor named Agostino di Duccio created beautiful pieces that are still admired by millions of people. But in one instance, he missed an opportunity because he couldn't visualize the end result.

The magnificent Basilica di Santa Maria del Fiore is the cathedral church of Florence, Italy. Construction began in 1296 and was completed in 1436, some 140 YEARS later. Agostino was commissioned to sculpt a giant statue of a Bible prophet for the cathedral.

A great piece of marble estimated to weigh between 12 and 14 tons was quarried and brought to Florence to create this colossal saint. The commission gave Agostino 18 months to complete the work, but after chiseling a large cavity in the mega block of marble, Agostino abandoned the project. His contract was terminated.

The marble block sat for the next 10 years until the commission found another sculptor, Antonio Rossellino, to carve the giant saint. He, too, failed. Another decade passed, then another. The commission even consulted da Vinci. Still, no sculpture.

Finally, 40 years after the first commissioning, 26-year-old Michelangelo Buonoratti offered to sculpt the giant saint. He worked for three years. Finally, one of the greatest sculptures ever created was complete: the David.

Michelangelo once said this about his works: "In every block of marble I see a statue as plain as though it stood before me, shaped and perfect in attitude and action. I have only to hew away the rough walls that imprison the lovely apparition to reveal it to the other eyes as mine see it."

Creating a vision is paramount to achieving what you want. Take the time to visualize. There really is a part of you that can create brilliant things, things that are just waiting to be released. At first your vision may seem like a fairy tale, but you can learn to focus on it in a way that will allow it to grow and take up space in your mind. Then, as its gravity starts to work for you, it will start to feel real.

I'm lucky to know Richard Brooke, author of three books and sought-after speaker. Richard coaches retreats on listening, vision, self-motivation, leadership, and action plans. He owns multiple successful businesses.

When Richard was young, he was on target to work his whole life at a chicken farm. Then he created a new vision, made it grow, and mastered the law of gravity in his life. He has become skilled at building successful businesses as well as people. He sets his sights on where he wants to be, gets a clear vision, makes a plan, and achieves it.

Richard teaches that when you keep reciting your vision to yourself, your subconscious mind (your spiritual, emotional, creative mind) hears it and begins to feel as though that vision has actually happened.

He explains, "The amount of time it takes is different for everybody, and it depends on what we're looking to take on, but somewhere between 30 and 100 movements, that powerful part of us starts to believe what we're telling it is true, and so it starts to dance in alignment with it."

Keep focusing on what you want. Do it 30, 40, 50, 100 times—enough that you believe it. Some things will take a while; others will come quickly. Don't be surprised if your conscious mind tries to stand in opposition to it. You might have thoughts like, *Oh, this is ridiculous. I've never done anything like this.* But if you keep feeding your vision, if you write it down and read it and reread it *out loud*, your creative mind starts to listen.

CLUED IN: JANET BRAY ATTWOOD

"When you are clear, what you want will show up in your life, and only to the extent that you are clear."

My youngest daughter came to me one morning and told me she'd dreamed that she was riding her bike without training wheels. "Do you know what that means?" I asked. "If you can dream it…" and she chimed in, "I can do it!"

So she and I went to the garage and started taking off those training wheels. Suddenly, my little girl got nervous. She said, "Dad, should we have a prayer?" I said, "Sure. Would you like to say it?" She said she would and started to pray, "Heavenly Father, please bless my bike not to be tricky."

Then she got on her bike. I helped her steady herself. On the second push, she was riding, just like she had seen herself do in her dream. She had thought about it enough, focused on it enough, that she could see it. It was real to her. And she did it.

In the book *Rich Dad, Poor Dad,* Robert Kiyosaki points out that you will find opportunities in the things that you study. He essentially asks, "Where do you spend your time?"

Think about that. What do your conversations consist of? What do you watch on TV? What kinds of books do you read? Where is your gravity heading? More importantly, where do you *want* it to be heading? If you're interested in a certain field, start studying it.

Let gravity pull you.

Stephenie was a young mother of three boys who found a life clue. Sixteen years had passed since she had earned her degree in English, and she was feeling like a "zombie" mom, stuck in a routine. The only job she had done was as a receptionist. She had thought about going to law school, but marriage and motherhood had changed her plans. Something was missing in her life, and she knew it.

Then, on June 2, 2003, a clue came to Stephenie in the form of a dream. Stephenie's dream was intense and vivid, and so unusual that she mused on her dream the entire day.

In her words in a nationally televised interview, she said, "Though I had a million things to do, I stayed in bed, thinking about the dream. Unwillingly, I eventually got up and did the immediate necessities, and then put everything that I possibly could on the back burner and sat down at the computer to write, something I hadn't done in so long that I wondered why I was bothering."

The idea of writing a story emerged in her mind. All day long, whatever she was doing, she built on the story of her dream in her mind. When the opportunity to sit down and begin writing it out appeared, she acted.

"The dream was just something I was so interested in, and it was so different from what my everyday was at the time. I just wanted to remember it so badly. That's why I started writing it down, not because I thought this would be a great story for a novel," Stephenie said.

As dreams usually are, it was a strange story, different and challenging. She kept quiet about it, fearing her husband of 15 years may think her a little weird. For this reason she did not share her story with anyone but her older sister. Writing it invigorated her and motivated her for the next three months until she finished her manuscript.

"Writing was a release. That was the dam bursting. I'd been bottling up who I was for so long, I needed an expression," said Stephenie.

She wrote her book for her own entertainment and escape. Her sister, however, encouraged her to send it out to agents for publication. She did, and she was met with failure. Of the 15 copies of her manuscript she sent to literary agents, five never replied. Nine flatly rejected her. Only one agent liked it.

Upon its release, Stephenie Meyer's *Twilight* was a hit. The dream that became a book in only three months shot to the top of the *New York Times* bestseller list. In 2006, the sequel book, *New Moon* was released and stayed in the number-one position on the bestseller list for six months. By the time the third novel, *Eclipse*, was finished, Stephenie was a worldwide phenomenon. On one book release, she sold over a million books in 24 hours.

Stephenie completed the series with a fourth book, *Breaking Dawn*. She has sold tens of millions of books, and her story has become a series of mega-hit Hollywood movies.

Stephenie did not set out to write a book and publish it. She simply followed thoughts and promptings that guided her to a new level of life and living. She felt compelled, and she didn't ignore those feelings. She didn't get too busy to pay attention to it. She found a way.

If something is important, and if we're willing to work at it, we can do the same. People who write books or work out or play beautiful music or have amazing-looking yards are not less busy than the rest of us. They're not excelling because they have extra time. They're excelling because they prioritize, they stick to what's important, and they feed that gravity. They put first what they're prompted to do. They make the time.

I bet that Stephenie Meyer's house was messy during the summer of 2003. Other things just weighed more in her mind at that time. She focused on those other things, and she brought them about.

Thoughts come into our minds for a reason. When you feel prompted to do something good, act on that prompting. Give it gravity. Let it pull you in the direction you need to go.

WIND IT UP

Think of something you want, and I mean something really great. Something you've wanted for years. Got it?

I bet at almost the same moment you thought about what you wanted, you also thought about why it isn't possible right now in your life.

Your reasons may be related to timing, money, location, family or work obligations, or simply disbelief in yourself. Anything can stand in the way and make you feel that you can't or shouldn't have it. The table on the next page is your first step in using gravity to turn that around.

In the left column, write down all those negative things that are pulling you away from being who you really want to be—thoughts like: I don't have enough money, I'm too old, I don't have the experience, I'm not organized—whatever phrases you're most likely to use to disqualify yourself any time you get an amazing idea or a moment of inspiration.

Now, for the right column. Here's where you write the exact opposite of what you see on the left. These are the reasons you *should* have this thing, whatever it is. If you wrote, "I lack experience," on the left, write something like, "I love learning new things," on the right.

As you draw those opposites, you might not believe your right column at first. It might not feel natural. That's because these positives are pulling you in a direction that is exactly opposite of where you've been facing.

The more you read your positives column, the more gravity it will gain. You can make these words become more and more empowering. You'll see how in Chapter 2.

Old Thinking	New Thinking

CHAPTER 2

THE POWER OF WORDS

Words create and change the world around you. Anything you can feel, whether good or bad, can be inspired by words. Words are like secret codes. They hold tremendous power. They can stir up hatred and defensiveness. They can evoke feelings of gratitude and love. One word can change your world for the better. Words are gifts that we give to others and to ourselves.

Words unlock power and open doors.

Think of a time (hopefully you have many to choose from) when someone thanked you or complimented you. No doubt those kind words lifted your mood and made you want to do even more things right.

I cannot tell you how much a card or a simple note can make my day. And what do we do with a card sent to us from someone who cared? We leave it out on the counter or post it up on the refrigerator. Then that single message sent just once is received over and over again, sometimes for a lifetime.

I once sat near a mom at a baseball tournament that my son was playing in. Her son was pitching, and as I listened to her cheer for him, I felt happy and excited. I took notes as fast as I could. Here are some of the things she was saying:

"You're in charge, Scott!"

"Here we go, Scott!"

"Nice pitch!"

"Let's go!"

"You're better than that!"

"Come on, Scott!"

"Get in the zone, buddy!"

"Right here!"

"That a-way, Scott!"

"Hang in there!"

"Keep it going, bud!"

"Nice work, Scott!"

Without a doubt, Scott knows he has an avid supporter, someone who is 100 percent on his side. He makes a mistake, and she doesn't tear him down; she reminds him that it's not typical. He can do better. She cheers for him as he tries and compliments him when he achieves. Words like that can become the motivation for us to reach deeper and find potentials we didn't even know were within us.

Words help create the dynamics of our relationships. Think about how it feels to say, "I love you." It's not always easy to utter those words, especially if you don't say them very often, but they can work magic.

An amazing couple in my neighborhood relies on that phrase. Jeff and his wife, Angela, both manage successful careers while raising three great kids. Jeff shared with me a clue on how they keep peace in their home. He said if they ever feel the tension start to rise, and it's evident that one of them is about to say something he or she might regret, they immediately tell the other person, "I love you." This instantly changes the mood and smoothes out the bumps. Those words somehow center them and help them see where they really want to be.

"I'm sorry" is another tough one, but once said, it delivers such a release that you wonder why you held onto it for so long. As soon as you let go of your pride and acknowledge your part in the problem, everything frees up for you, and more often than not, the relationship improves.

The thing with words (and we all know this) is that it takes more time and effort to build up than it does to tear down. Our obligation to those around us is to be aware and to conscientiously build.

> I watched them tearing a building down,
> A gang of men in this busy town,
> With a ho-heave-ho and a lusty yell,
> They swung a beam and a side wall fell.

> And I asked the foreman, "Are these men skilled?"
> (The men he'd hire if he had had to build?)

He gave a laugh and said, "No, indeed!
Just a common laborer is all I need.

I can easily wreck in a day or two
What builders have taken a year to do."
I asked myself as I went my way,
"Which of these roles have I tried to play?

Am I a builder who works with care,
Measuring life with rule and square?
Or am I a wrecker as I walk the town,
Content with the labor of tearing down?"

– Unknown

Study people who are good at building relationships using positive and encouraging words. They'll be the people you're naturally drawn to because they make you feel good about yourself. Strive to master what they do, starting with giving at least one compliment each day. Practice on people you know and on people you don't.

Feel it, and it means more.

The most meaningful words are not necessarily the most eloquent or well-chosen ones. Sincerity gives words unique power that can come in no other way. True emotion always shows through.

In the 1930s, actor and orator Charles Laughton was known for the readings and recitations he performed. He was attending church one Sunday when he was asked if he would recite the 23rd Psalm. He generously agreed, and in his well-known and articulate voice, he stood up and amazed the congregation with an extemporaneous performance that commanded a standing ovation.

The 23rd Psalm was also the favorite of Mr. Pleasant, an elderly member of the congregation who had a speech impediment and could only mumble most of his words. As the applause for Laughton died, Mr. Pleasant stood and walked to the front of the chapel. There he, too, would offer his recital of the famous psalm.

The congregation silently blushed for him, wondering if perhaps the old gentleman did not realize he was about to follow one of the greatest speakers of the time.

Mr. Pleasant folded his arms, looked upward, and began to recite the psalm, his labored words reverberating with humility. When he finished his rendition, he respectfully limped back to his seat. The chapel was reverent. Silence; no applause. Only sniffles from the emotionally touched congregation. Even the pastor wept.

Later that day at the Sunday luncheon, a woman respectfully asked Mr. Laughton what he thought about his standing ovation and how it contrasted with Mr. Pleasant moving people to tears. Mr. Laughton, pondering his response, said, "I've thought of nothing else since it happened. I, too, have wondered why. I believe it is because I know the 23rd Psalm, but Mr. Pleasant knows the Good Shepherd."

"I've learned that people will forget what you said, people will forget what you did, but people will never forget how you made them feel."

When a feeling precedes an expression, words become secondary. Much can be said with eye contact. Babies can tell you without words exactly what they need from you, whether they coo at you to invite you to play or fuss so you'll pick them up. People are persuaded far more by what they feel than by words they actually hear.

This can take the fear out of talking about critical subjects. You don't have to worry so much about how to approach a subject. Your sincere, genuine feelings carry more weight than the actual words you use.

Be good to yourself.

There's a saying that I love:

Watch your thoughts, for they become words.
Watch your words, for they become actions.
Watch your actions, for they become habits.
Watch your habits, for they become character.
Watch your character, for it becomes your destiny.

The words you think and say to yourself are powerful. They can be both dangerous and empowering. We've all had days when we've looked in the mirror and thought, *Ugly*. Or maybe we're working on a difficult project, and we think, *Stupid*. Or we stumble and think, *Klutz!* Sometimes we even say those things to ourselves out loud.

Now, let me ask you, would you ever speak that way to a friend? To your child? To anyone you care about? Of course you wouldn't! It's horrifying to imagine being so rude and condescending to anyone. Doesn't it seem wrong that we have moments when we're willing to treat ourselves that way?

Learn to talk positively to yourself. Get along with yourself. Like yourself. Treat yourself as though you're the most important person you know. What you say to yourself affects how you think and how others think of you.

What we expect in ourselves and in others continually manifests itself in the words we use. Consciously change the words you use to describe your activities. Focus on the reason you will succeed, not how you could fail. The more you do this, the more real the thing you are after will become. When you start to believe there is a real payoff, you will naturally work harder, you'll enjoy the journey, and you're more likely to succeed.

Look at those around you who have their acts together. Maybe they're successful in business or in their relationships. Maybe they're good at reaching goals. Notice that these people use assertive words, even if they're doing something simple, like ordering a sandwich. It's not, "Can I have…?" It's, "I'll have."

This same attitude shows when they're doing something difficult, like training for a marathon. You won't hear, "I'm trying to get ready for a race." Rather, they'll say, "I'm running a marathon in June." They talk as though they're already there.

If you feel like people aren't responding to you the way you'd like, pay attention to your words. You might be influencing them to treat you that way. You write your own price tag, and you wear it.

Once I was in line behind a man ordering his meal at a fast food place. Here's how he placed his order: "Why don't you give me a double cheeseburger?" It's possible the girl taking his order might have thought, *Because it will make you fat*, or *Because they don't pay me enough*. This particular individual had chosen words that placed him in the inferior position. His words asked for a *no*.

I really believe that you can assert your worth by speaking positively to yourself. I've had occasion to teach this word power to my kids.

Not too long ago, my oldest daughter was unhappy in her job. Although she was making pretty good money, she just didn't feel right about the service the company she worked for was providing. She confided, "I don't know if I like it, Dad."

"OK," I said. "Before you quit, though, have something else lined up." She said she'd been looking but she couldn't find anything that paid as well.

So she and I worked on a vision statement together. Not a goal; goal statements only confirm that you do not have the thing you desire. A vision statement, on the other hand, is written from your point of view, as though you already have it. It's worded as if it is so, and you have to give it as much color and feeling as you can.

My daughter was bold with hers. She wrote down what kind of job she wanted, what skills it would help her build, what it would pay, and a date by which she would have it. She gave herself one month, and she was diligent. She read that thing every day, morning and night. I saw how crumpled up it was; it was well worn.

It only took her about 10 days to land a fantastic job in an entirely different industry. Not only that, but it was a job that is usually only offered to existing employees within the company. She had actually passed over that requirement to get to the position.

When you put your vision down on paper and then repeat it in your own words with as much feeling as you can, it becomes a molding experience. You act differently. You perform differently. You expect it. You get where you want to go faster.

Land your point.

On any given day, we say and hear far more words than necessary. If I share only a few words with you, I can inspire you and make you think, simply because of the power behind them. Here are some examples:

I have a dream.
Ask not what your country can do for you.
Thou shalt not…
One small step for man, one giant leap for mankind.
Come, follow me.

Notice how each small set of words takes you somewhere in your mind, reminds you, or clues you into a teacher or a person or a place. Each phrase can make you feel something. That is the strength of a few well-placed words.

You'll see that clue over and over in people who don't say much. When they do speak, they don't waste words. They get right to the point, say it once, and their comment is usually worth something.

It's just the opposite with those who chatter. We all know people who flutter around and around but just can't seem to land on the point. They can't even engage the landing gear. It can be frustrating to listen to these people, whether they're a friend who called you on the phone or a speaker at a workshop. It's hard not to think, *Get to the point! Just say what you want to say! Land the plane!*

It may take practice, but it's important to learn to say more with less. It's an indication that you know what you want. People will notice and appreciate you at a higher level.

Think of the Gettysburg Address, that brief yet famous speech by Abraham Lincoln. Right? Wrong. The Gettysburg Address was actually a two-hour oration by Edward Everett, a highly educated, well-respected politician of the time. He had been a strong voice in support of the Lincoln administration and the cause of liberty for slaves. At Gettysburg, he gave a stirring speech, perhaps the most important address of his life and career.

When the applause subsided, a tired old gentleman approached the podium as the second speaker. He spoke for only two minutes, including five interruptions for applause. Abraham Lincoln's remarks were officially only the presidential remarks that followed the Gettysburg Address, but his words that day were so profound that the speech has endured as the greatest American address ever given. Today we all ascribe the title of the Gettysburg Address to Mr. Lincoln.

Even Edward Everett himself acknowledged that Lincoln's brief words had eclipsed his own. The day following the Gettysburg event, he wrote a note to the president that read, "I should be glad if I could flatter myself that I came as near to the central idea of the occasion, in two hours, as you did in two minutes."

Abraham Lincoln, through hard study and practice, became a master of profound brevity. He could not only develop and make a point in one or two sentences, he could carry his message on the wings of authority or humor directly to the heart of understanding.

WIND IT UP

The very first concept in this book is a powerful one: The Law of Gravity. Remember the Old Thinking column, where you listed your self-limiting beliefs, and how one by one, you rooted out everything that's holding you back? You listed all the reasons you will become the person you are meant to be with a converse list in the New Thinking column.

You now have the ingredients to write your very own vision statement. In the lines below, start writing the things from the New Thinking column. Go in any order. Be as clear and as colorful as you possibly can. Do not worry about punctuation or sentence structure. This is *your* vision statement.

Now, for the next 30 days, read it to yourself morning and night. This is important. Habits form over time, and most people drop off after a week or so. Give this one at least 30 days, and see what power your own words can tap into.

_____

_____

_____

_____

_____

_____

_____

CHAPTER 3

PRACTICE MAKES YOU LUCKY

This chapter is for those of you who have seen a successful person and thought, *Man, is he ever lucky!* Guess what. He isn't. It's never just luck. Success takes hours and hours of effort, and there are no shortcuts.

Being successful at something, whether it's speaking in public, keeping your cool in intense situations, or performing any specific skill, takes hours of practice. According to the research done by Malcom Gladwell, author of *Outliers*, it takes 10,000 hours to master a skill. That's the equivalent practice time of doing a full-time job for about five years.

Mozart's earliest concerto that's considered a masterpiece was composed when he was 21 years old. He had already been composing concertos for ten years. Similarly, when the Beatles burst onto the music scene in 1964 to seemingly instant success, they had already given an estimated 1,200 live performances.

Greatness takes practice. Do you know what that much practice does to a human being? It makes you ready. It gives you confidence. It makes you feel like you deserve success—because you do.

Legend has it that Pablo Picasso was sketching in the park when a bold woman approached him. She recognized the great artist and insisted he sketch her portrait.

Picasso agreed. After studying his subject for a moment, he used a single pencil stroke to create her portrait. He handed the woman his work.

"It's amazing!" she gushed. "You managed to capture my essence with one stroke, in one moment. Thank you! How much do I owe you?"

"Five thousand dollars," the artist replied.

The woman was stunned. "How could you want so much money for this picture?" she gasped. "It only took you a few seconds to draw it!"

Picasso responded, "Madame, it took me my entire life."

What do you want right now in your life? How much time and effort have you consistently practiced that thing? Are you willing to put in some hours?

I'm not talking about dabbling in something interesting. I don't mean that you should find something that will entertain you, something that you might fiddle with for a while, something you'll pick up and put down.

The difference between practicing and fiddling is commitment. What are you willing to sacrifice?

CLUED IN: HENRY WADSWORTH LONGFELLOW

"The heights by great men reached and kept, were not obtained by sudden flight. But they, while their companions slept, were toiling upward in the night."

World-class boxer Larry Holmes was not a fiddler. He didn't dabble. He won the first 48 of his professional fights. Yes, that's in a row. This feat landed him one step behind the greatest record of all time set by Rocky Marciano, who won the first 49 of his fights. But Holmes was probably the most unlikely champion in the history of the sport.

He was born in the South in 1949, the fourth of twelve children in a poor family. When Larry was five years old, the family moved 1,000 miles north to the steel mills, foundries, and factories of Easton, Pennsylvania, where they hoped to make a better life. But Larry's father was unable to find a job in their new location and ended up moving on alone to Connecticut while the rest of the family remained in poverty back in Easton.

Larry took his first job when he was in the first grade, shining shoes for 15 cents with the hope of a tip. By the seventh grade, he dropped out of school to make a dollar an hour working in a carwash.

Larry loved athletics, but because he had quit school, he missed opportunities to play sports. He started fighting in backroom boxing matches, street brawls, and alley fights, which provided entertainment and sometimes free food. It also got him 13 days in juvenile detention.

Eventually, Larry began boxing with a local athletic association, where his trainer had him spar with some of the toughest fighters in New York and Philadelphia. Larry practiced the basics over and over until they became an instinct to him: Keep your guard up. Don't drop your hand after a punch. Keep your eye on your opponent, even when you get hit.

After some amateur fights, Larry participated in the Olympic trials but was met with a disqualification. He returned to the practice ring where he was pitted to spar against professionals who were either superstars or were on their way to stardom: Jimmy Young, Ernie Shavers, Smokin' Joe Frazier, and Muhammad Ali.

Larry would later relate, "I thought, *Hey, if I can hold my own against these guys, what about later?*" Joe Frazier sparred with Holmes in preparation for a fight with Ali. Holmes commented that Frazier took his anger out on him.

The big pros would hit him so hard that Larry learned to move away from their power and lure them into his ever-improving left jab. That move became Holmes's weapon after a devastating right-thumb fracture that required surgery, pins, and a full cast. He kept practicing anyway, and eventually he could strike a left jab in nineteen-hundredths of a second, the time it takes to blink your eye. Holmes claimed two of his first 48 undefeated bouts as "one-armed" victories.

Revered today as one of the greatest fighters of all time, Larry Holmes held the second longest championship title in history (behind Joe Louis), with seven and a half years and 20 title defenses. He fought 75 professional fights against some of the toughest names in the business, earning 69 wins and 44 knockouts. He had more KOs than most professional fighters have total bouts.

"People think that I reached the top overnight," Holmes observed. "Well, it took me 14 years. I was 29 before I really made it. I've had my jaws and hands broken. One arm is out of place. I've paid my dues in this business…I always felt good about myself. I was just an average person. I always felt I could do anything anyone else could. If an average person makes up their mind to do something, they can."

CLUED IN: BRUCE LEE

"I fear not the man who has practiced 10,000 kicks once, but I fear the man who has practiced one kick 10,000 times."

Lucky people have a secret: they work. Thomas Jefferson said, "I find that the harder I work, the more luck I seem to have." It's true. Hard work and practice prepare you for the moment. And when that moment comes, the time for preparation is over. You're either ready for the opportunity or you're not.

Find something you love, and do it. Then keep doing it. Successful people aren't necessarily successful because they're smarter or more talented. Their natural talents may have given them a head start, but practice made the rest of the difference. Hard work is the bulk of the advantage.

Becoming an expert requires practice. It's often mundane, but use the vision of the end as the fuel to push through the repetition you need to master what you want to achieve. Realize that everything is difficult in the middle. But having a clear image of what you want will pull you through and sustain you. If you love something, want it, and have a passion for it, you will enjoy it and work at it, and it will serve you.

Remember the movie *A League of Their Own?* It's about a women's baseball league that started during World War II to fill the gap left in baseball when so many players were drafted. In the movie, Geena Davis plays Dottie Hinson, the star player and the leader and unifier for her team. During the season, Dottie's husband is wounded in the war and gets sent home. Naturally, she wants to be with him and finally resolves to leave the team.

Watch the Clip

When she tells her coach, played by Tom Hanks, that it's just too hard, he gives her what I believe is a brilliant clue: "It's *supposed* to be hard. If it wasn't hard, everyone would do it. The hard is what makes it great."

Honestly, can you think of anything great that comes easily? Whether it's accomplishing an athletic achievement or a business goal, being a great parent, keeping a clean house, going back to college—anything worthwhile—it's hard. And being hard is what makes it fulfilling to achieve.

It always takes willpower to stick to what you're going after. But here's another clue: The best way to ensure success is to ritualize it. Want more willpower? Turn it into a habit. As you form habits, your brain changes and new neurological pathways are created. The more frequent the action, the stronger the habit. The stronger the habit, the more automatic your actions and performance become.

Discipline now means freedom later.

Opportunities come all the time, every day, and if you are prepared, they are yours. If you're not prepared, they do not belong to you. This is true everywhere—the workplace, financial opportunities, education.

You may feel discouraged as you sock your money away if you focus on the many fun things you could do with it. But if you stick to your plan, you will have the resources for investment opportunities that come. Or, in a simpler scenario, you'll be able to take advantage of sale prices on items you've been looking for. Conversely, if you take the privilege before it belongs to you, if you buy what you want on credit when you don't have the money to back up the purchase, you're shackled to that item until you pay it off. No freedom.

In high school, if you study when everyone else is playing video games or going to the movies, you will have more choices when it comes to choosing where to go to college; you may even earn a scholarship. In college, work translates into internships, letters of recommendation, and networking opportunities. And those opportunities mean freedom.

This clue applies to everything in life, whether you're going the extra mile at work, trying to learn all you can, or doing something more personal like counting calories and getting more exercise. Your choices and opportunities increase when you're willing to work at something. Even if it's just the freedom to look great in any outfit or physically do any activity you're interested in.

By the way, extra responsibilities at work are like free education. Jump at the chance to build experience, and don't always look for extra pay.

Just try to become the most valuable person around. Extra work is an opportunity that creates future opportunities.

My cousin Jim Thayer played professional football as a kicker. My uncle told him, "Be so good that they'll have no choice but to use you." To get that good, Jim knew he had to not only practice but to make his practice hard. He always kicked into the wind. He would visualize goal posts in the hallway and practice kicking into a space that was only an armspan. Taking his dad's advice to heart and putting in the practice paid off. Jim played many years in the NFL doing what he loved.

Learn what your conscience tells you to learn; work at what it says to work at. Then when opportunities come, you're ready. You're not left wishing you knew how. Decide what you want, and don't stop practicing.

CLUED IN: JOHN HANLEY

"Chance favors the prepared mind."

WIND IT UP

Here's a fun exercise you can do right now to prove to yourself that you can do something challenging. Say the first three letters of the alphabet out loud: *ABC*. Now, say them in reverse: *CBA*. Do that a couple of times until you can quickly say, *ABCCBA*. You now have mastered the first three letters of the alphabet forward and backward.

Next, add one letter: *D. ABCD, DCBA*. Repeat it over and over. Continue the process, and in less than one day, you will fluently be able to say the alphabet forward and backward. Try it! You'll have developed a skill that is both amazing and fun—plus you can dazzle people at parties.

More importantly, it will take your mind back to that wonderful time when you had to memorize things. You started doing it in grade school, remember? Perhaps it was the preamble to the Constitution or a poem or your multiplication tables. We did it in our early school years, and your brain will love you if you continue to exercise those memorization muscles.

CHAPTER 4

THE HAPPINESS FACTOR

No matter how hard life gets, I'm convinced that everyone can find something to be grateful for. And no matter how good life is, anyone can find something to be bitter about. Somewhere along the line, you just have to choose. Are you going to be positive or are you going to be negative? When you're thankful for what you have, what you have is enough.

See things differently, and things will become different.

You can have a horrible day at the beach, and you can have a great day doing yard work. How you see it is up to you. When you look at things differently, things become different. You become different. When you act grateful, you become more grateful, and you begin to recognize more of the things in your life that are good.

Most people don't set out to be negative, but we are naturally built to scan our environments for danger so we may avoid the pitfalls. Just as we instinctively look for danger, we can train ourselves to scan for the good in everyday situations.

Viktor Frankl, an Austrian psychiatrist and neurologist who spent two and a half years in a Nazi concentration camp, wrote a great book called *Man's Search for Meaning.* In this book, Frankl talks about using words to find the happy side of life. Often people can find meaning in their lives through joyful things like love or something they've created or something they've worked to achieve.

Happiness doesn't require a theme park. You don't have to have external things or material possessions to be happy. Regardless of what's happening in your life, you can be at peace about the way you act.

There can also be meaning, even peace, in suffering. That's a tough one for most of us because we think we're not allowed to feel sorrow; we need to keep a stiff upper lip, have a positive attitude, and look on the bright side. But Frankl explains that you just need to be true in your suffering. Sometimes things happen that cause sorrow in our lives, and the question is, do we handle those things with grace and dignity?

Everything can be taken from a man but one thing. The last human freedom is to choose your own attitude in any given set of circumstances, to choose your own way.

When you practice noticing, commenting on, even writing down the good things that happen to you, you train your mind to notice more opportunities. You start to scan the world for positives, and you become happier, more grateful, and more optimistic.

"A loving person lives in a loving world. A hostile person lives in a hostile world. Everyone you meet is your mirror."

I had an experience that helped me grasp this principle. In the late 1990s, my family and I were going through a rough time financially. I had been unwise with our income, and we found ourselves living beyond our means. Month after month, the debt became worse. As crazy as it sounds, we had gotten to where we were living off our credit cards for the basic needs of life. I can still remember going through the grocery line, worried that our card might be declined.

Day after day, I stressed over how I was going to get out of the mess I was in. I was angry with myself, and I was angry with others whom I thought had mistreated me. We had sold one of our cars, our home, and eventually we started selling our furniture just to provide our basic needs. My health was poor. I was at one of the lowest points of my life.

Then one afternoon, I remember driving in my car, looking out the window, and wondering, "How bad is this going to get?" Then I saw something that made a huge difference in how I was seeing things. Off to my right on the sidewalk sat a group of people, including a man with no arms. He was drinking a soda. How? He placed his feet in a cupping shape and lifted the cup and straw to his mouth. I watched him do this as he laughed and smiled, carrying on a conversation.

To watch him, you would have thought he hadn't a care in the world. Here I was thinking I couldn't handle another ounce of discouragement, and this man had no arms or hands, and he was happy.

Was it because of the friends who surrounded him? Was it the fresh air in his lungs? Was it the beautiful blue sky or the warmth of the sun? I had all of those same gifts but couldn't see any of them. Why? Because I was so focused on what I had lost that I had stopped being grateful for what I had.

As soon as I started counting my blessings, I began to look at my life through a different set of lenses. I started rolling up my own ball of string, finding my way, and recognizing how many things I had to be grateful for. I started thinking, *Wow, I guess my problems aren't so bad. I am being blessed.* I had just forgotten.

CLUED IN: ALBERT EINSTEIN

"There are only two ways to live your life. One is as though nothing is a miracle. The other is as though everything is a miracle."

Be grateful.

A key factor in choosing to be happy is to look at things positively. Count your blessings. Being grateful reveals the joy in any circumstance you may find yourself in. Expressing gratitude is the way to stay grateful. Start and end every day on your knees. Learn the power of *thank you.*

The late Cavett Robert was a popular motivational speaker and the founder of the National Speakers Association. He used to tell the story of how he learned the hard way about taking time to appreciate life.

He was at a speaking engagement, and the meeting had run overtime, jeopardizing his chances of catching his flight home. Cavett completed his speech in the grand ballroom of the Fairmont Hotel in New Orleans, then rushed through the convention center and ran to catch the next elevator going down to the ground level.

Once on the elevator, he tapped the "G" button repeatedly, hoping it would hurry the process of closing the doors. As soon as it began its descent, he checked his watch. He could still make his flight if there were no delays with the elevator or the taxi. Just when he thought his luck was going to hold, he felt the elevator slowing for the third floor.

The doors opened, and no one was there. *Hurry up!* he thought to himself. Hearing someone coming, he impatiently called out, "Hurry— elevator going down!" Then he saw the red tip of a white cane tap-tap into the doorway.

"I'm sorry; I'll be right there," came a humble response. Cavett was crushed with humiliation. As the doors closed, not knowing how to handle the hollow silence, he asked, "Well, how are you today, sir?" His voice was now shaky and embarrassed. The reply came like a heavy blow to his soul: "Grateful, my friend. Grateful."

Cavett Robert, the great teacher and motivator, was humbled to the dust. Suddenly missing an elevator, a taxi, or even a flight seemed trivial. He would later state, "While in my rude haste I was so caught up in my self-gratification and not an attitude of gratitude that I found myself cursing the light as this gentle man was blessing the darkness."

He said he was never the same after that experience. In his prayers he asked for help to always realize how important a grateful attitude is in life.

There's significance in the fact that he prayed for help with this. Human nature pulls us toward being proud of what we've accomplished. We like to think, ungratefully, that we did it ourselves. We tend to look out for ourselves, making sure our own needs are met. It takes conscientious, daily effort to remain grateful and recognize life's gifts.

You can do this through prayer or by writing down three or five or more things you're grateful for. Create a reporting system. If you choose prayer, ask for help in the morning, and give thanks at night and report on how you did. If you're making a list, set out to find things to be grateful for, and write down what those are. Thank people for the influence they are in your life. Do it every day.

Be happy.

Remember that one-hit wonder from 1988, "Don't Worry, Be Happy?" It topped the music charts at number one and earned Bobby McFerrin a Grammy for Song of the Year. Everybody knew that song. Not everybody wanted to admit that they loved it, but I know I'm not the only one who turned it up and started singing when I was alone in my car.

It wasn't just because of the catchy tune. That song had an important message: be happy. Even when things go wrong—your rent is late, you've got no cash, no style, and no girl to make you smile—be happy. The message was not to *let* something happy happen to you. It wasn't even to *make* something happy happen to you. It was way more proactive than that: Make the decision to be happy, and be happy.

It's a message that resonates with people because we all know on some level that being happy is good for us. It changes us beyond simply being in a good mood. It's healthy for the body, it establishes stronger relationships, it makes us look more attractive, and we get treated better by society.

Being happy begins with deciding to be happy. It can take practice. You might need to write it down as a vision statement or put a sticky note on your fridge to remind yourself at first, but the habit will form, and you will change.

The world is kinder to happy people.

I recently experienced the power of being happy on a family vacation to Disneyland and California Adventure. There was a day when we got to the park a little bit late, and the place was incredibly busy. The lines were long, and all the fast passes were gone. Our kids seemed discouraged.

We went over to the information desk at California Adventure to find out if any rides had fast passes left. None did. But here's what I didn't realize I was doing. I was smiling and having a great time, even though my kids were a little bit bummed. There was a band playing, and the beat was making me bounce. I was doing a little dance while we waited in line. I was having a good time. My kids were almost a little bit embarrassed because I was so dang happy on purpose. But there was no way I was going to act disappointed. I was smiling.

When it was my turn, I walked up to the desk and said, "We are so excited to be here. Will you give us some fast passes?" The guy said, "Unfortunately, there aren't any left. It's just a busy day today." I can't remember what I said next, but my attitude didn't change. Then he said,

"Because you're so happy, I'm going to give you some fast passes. What ride do you want to go on right now?"

He pulled out of his desk these little cards, wrote his signature on them, and gave me enough for the six of us. We walked over to Tower of Terror, which had a 100-minute wait, and got right on.

My point is that I was so happy, there was nothing that was going to make me sad, and things went my way. Will it always work? No. Things aren't always going to go your way. But you up your chances when you're happy.

Author and speaker John Maxwell says, "If people get along with you, they will go along with you." If I had said, "You don't have any fast passes, do you?" I have no doubt I would have gotten a no.

Act positively by smiling and being happy. Your words will be happy. People will respond. The world will treat you better, and you'll achieve more. In fact, those who smile are more likely to be promoted, and they're more likely to be approached. Put on a smile at meetings and appointments, and people will react to you more advantageously.

Happiness improves you.

Happiness is something you cultivate. You create it within yourself and initiate it in others. And it can actually contribute to success. According to Shawn Achor, author of *The Happiness Advantage*, each of us has a range of success, based on our own ability or potential. Science has proven that happy people perform at the top of that range. Achor explains that "happiness is the center around which success orbits." Achor gives some interesting examples:

- Doctors who are in a good mood show almost three times more intelligence and creativity while making diagnoses than doctors in a neutral state, and they make those diagnoses 19 percent faster.

- Optimistic salespeople outsell their pessimistic counterparts by 56 percent.

- Students primed to feel happy before taking math achievement tests far outperform their neutral peers.

Whatever you set out to do, if you're happy, you'll do it better.

Smiling is healthy.

One of the first things I noticed and loved about my wife, Jackie, was her great sense of humor. I love her laugh. I love her smile. Decades later, I still love those things about her.

People need laughter in their lives. When you smile, you draw people to you. Research shows that people who smile are more stable, enjoy happier marriages, get along better with others, and live longer.

Smiles establish trust. What do we do with babies and little children? We smile at them constantly, a key factor in bonding. All people, no matter what age, foster rapport with smiles. It's a way of saying, "I see you. I care about you. You matter to me."

A study in Norway followed 54,000 people for seven years. These people were asked about their sense of humor and how often they laugh. Those that found the world the most funny were 35 percent less likely to die during the study period.

Perhaps that can be explained by the fact that smiling relieves stress. It actually lowers your blood pressure and releases endorphins and serotonin, the body's natural feel-good factors.

Because stress can show up in our faces, smiling helps prevent us from looking tired, worn down, and overwhelmed. Have you heard the saying, *A smile is an inexpensive way to change your looks*? It's true!

When you're not feeling particularly happy, try smiling. You'll actually feel it starting to trick your body into feeling happier. It's almost impossible to feel sad or to think negative thoughts when you're smiling. People can tell you're smiling even when you're on the phone; you just sound different. That smile affects your tone of voice and even what you say.

A smile is a gift.

We each need to see someone's face light up when we walk into the room. Don't you find that you gravitate toward people who are happy to see you? Whether it's your baby who can't contain his excitement that you're home or a good friend whom you just bumped into at the post office, a heartfelt, happy greeting can make your day.

I've seen this in action with my friend Sean Murphy. He's a business consultant who travels the world speaking and training. Off and on we see each other at events. Sean is never alone. He's a magnet. People just want to be around him. He always has a smile on his face. He's a great listener. When you shake his hand, he asks, "How are you?" and he really wants to know.

Sometimes I barely get to talk to Sean because of the crowd that surrounds him. Why do people flock to him? Because everyone in the room is thinking the same thing: *I'm going to feel better about myself in about five seconds. I'm going to go talk to Sean.*

Never underestimate the power of your smile.

WIND IT UP

So, what are you grateful for? Who are you grateful for? Start right now to retrain your brain to look for possibilities. Write down five things you consider miracles in your life. Go ahead, get a pen. I'm serious. Write down at least five miracles. Close your eyes and smile as you think of them. Then write down at least five people for whom you are grateful. (Careful. You might get going and run out of room.)

Now send them a note or a card and tell them. Not an e-mail or a text. They're worth more than that. Sending someone a physical thank-you will strengthen your relationship and put a smile on both your faces.

Miracles   People

_____   _____

_____   _____

_____   _____

_____   _____

_____   _____

_____   _____

_____   _____

_____   _____

CHAPTER 5

WHAT GOES IN

MUST COME OUT

Have you ever looked out a window into the bright sunlight or watched a camera flash, then closed your eyes? On the back of your eyelids, you see an outline of what you have just looked at. That image, what science calls a cognitive after-image, remains with us. When we focus mentally on something for a long period of time, even if it's not an actual image, the effect on the mind is the same. Thoughts stay with us. We create new neural pathways, actual new connections in the brain, that change the way we see things and the way we do things.

You become what you focus on.

Every minute nearly a thousand milliliters of blood flow through your brain. This amazing organ has 100 billion neurons sending rapid-fire messages that tell you what you see, hear, feel, and taste. Your organs function. You move. You perceive. You think. You connect thoughts. You remember.

But memory, over time, can fade. Have you ever been reminded of something, and thought, *Oh my gosh, I totally forgot about that,* and you have the feeling that you may never have thought of it again if someone hadn't brought it up? Long-term memory is remarkably stable, but it takes effort to keep important things at the front of the mind.

Because we are constantly acquiring, processing, and organizing information, we have a lot stored away. There's just no way to be aware of all of it, all the time. So we leave it in long-term memory and call it up when we need it. To keep something in awareness, we have to consciously focus on it. Only then can we allow it to impact how we live each day.

The amazing facet of the brain that allows us to do this is called the reticular activating system (RAS). This is how we can disregard things that are not relevant while focusing on things that are. Without it, or when it's not working right, we would all seem to have attention deficit disorder. We'd turn our heads and look at every stimulus that came our way. We'd notice every car that drove by. We'd constantly be distracted by the air conditioning or the noise the computer makes. We would hear background conversations in crowds. We'd smell everything, look at everything, hear everything. It would be too much information to sort out.

But the RAS allows us to focus, to filter out what's not vital and concentrate on what is. This is what gives each of us the ability to keep what is most important at the front of our minds. It's how we focus on and eventually achieve what we want, so we have to pay attention to what we're thinking about. What are we putting our time and energy into? Then we must ask ourselves, "Is this OK? Is this what I want to achieve?"

You can use the reticular activating system to your advantage: feed your mind the things you want to focus on, and do it often enough that those things don't fade. It takes a little effort, but it's really not hard.

One thing you can do to focus on what's important to you is spend time every day reading or listening to books or lectures on areas of your life you want to improve. Reading just 10 pages at a time, or listening to 10 or 20 minutes of audio while you're driving in your car will add up faster than you think. If you carve out just 20 minutes to listen to books or lectures about the subjects you want to improve on (and you really don't even have to carve it out—the average person spends an hour and a half in the car every day), it will equal 86 hours of self-improvement every year. And that's if you only do it on weekdays! That's like going to five or six seminars. If you do this, I promise you will not be the same person a year from now.

You are what you eat.

The body is more intricate than most of us can imagine. In only a square inch of skin, there are 20 feet of blood vessels. We use 200 different muscles just to take one step. Blood travels 60,000 miles a day as it courses through the body. Many little body parts function together, doing things we're not even aware of, to keep us going every second.

You'll look at food differently when you start to really believe that what goes into your body is what comes out. You'll see it in the way you feel, how clearly you think, and how well your body performs. Your objective in choosing what to eat will no longer be just to feel full but to find food that offers the greatest dividends. When you make this realization, you'll find yourself planning ahead, choosing the right kind of snacks and meals.

Foods themselves give us clues to health. Many nutritionists believe that foods can show you by the way they look which part of the body they're good for. It's kind of fun to take a look at what food can reveal.

A sliced carrot has the pattern of a pupil with an iris. The carrot gets its orange color from beta-carotene, which is transformed in the body to vitamin A. And vitamin A helps form rhodopsin, which helps us see in poor lighting.

A tomato is red and has four chambers, just like the heart. Lycopene, a source of antioxidants and the very thing that helps make the tomato red, also helps prevent the formation of oxidized LDL cholesterol (the "bad" cholesterol) in the blood.

The womb-shaped avocado contains essential fatty acids and B vitamins, both of which contribute to the metabolism of hormones. Interestingly, it takes nine months for an avocado to grow from a blossom to a ripe fruit.

A walnut looks just like the brain, with hemispheres and wrinkles, even divisions that resemble the cerebrum and cerebellum. Walnuts are a great source of omega-3 essential fatty acids, which promote better cognitive function. A quarter-cup of walnuts provides over 90 percent of the daily value for these essential fatty acids.

Are you starting to see that nature provides its own clues? Even if you don't want to play the "what does this food look like?" game, you can be confident that what nature provides is good for the body. Eat a variety of natural, unprocessed foods, and your body will get the nutrients it needs.

Eat what you need.

Remember when you were a kid and felt proud when you were in the clean-plate club? You were praised for eating everything on your plate, and you got a little lecture about starving kids in Africa when you didn't. Oh, yeah, and you didn't get dessert until you cleaned your plate either! How crazy is that? Overeat, and then you can enjoy some extra, empty calories.

The challenge in our culture is that this training sinks in and carries over into adulthood. We've got this mindset that we have to eat everything that's set before us. It's rude and wasteful if we don't.

The truth is our bodies have been sending us clues our whole lives that tell us just how much food we need. Initially we paid attention to those clues, at least until we were about two years old. We stopped eating when we were full, turning our heads and leaning back in our high chairs when we felt satisfied—even if it was our favorite food. And if Mom insisted we take one more bite, we spit it out!

But at age two, we began to pleasure eat. Somehow we learned to ignore the body when it says, "I'm full!" Now we want to finish what we start. We push past the full signal because it tastes good or because the party's still going on or because we're still sitting in the restaurant or because someone made it especially for us. But guess what. People are not as offended as you think they'll be if you don't eat it all. And having another slice of pizza will do nothing for children in Africa or anywhere else in the world.

Here's a life-changing clue. As soon as you start to feel slightly full, slow down and stop eating. You're not hungry anymore! Save the rest for later. I know a 69-year-old woman, a mother of seven, who has always kept herself trim. She never eats until she's full; only until the edge is gone. Her motto: "I'd rather see it go to waste than to my waist."

Don't get me wrong; we all eat for enjoyment. I'm not taking that away. But when you really understand and experience that what goes in is what comes out, you'll pleasure-eat in moderation. You'll be looking for those four or five servings of fresh fruits and vegetables that take up a lot of room in your stomach and don't leave much space for junk. If you follow the 80/20 rule, you'll eat high-energy, feel-good foods at least 80 percent of the time and go for the fun foods 20 percent (or less) of the time.

Work harder, last longer.

It's true that the human body is an amazing machine, but that's such an understatement. The body is so much more. Even the best machine ever built will break down from hard work. The more miles you put on your car, the closer it comes to being junked.

Unlike a man-made machine, the body doesn't wear out with exercise; it becomes stronger with harder tasks. Muscle builds. Lung capacity increases. Blood pressure decreases. Sleep becomes more efficient. The more you work it, the better your body performs and the longer it will last.

Exercise releases pleasure-inducing chemicals called endorphins, the body's natural anti-depressants. You become more alert. Working out can actually increase your IQ for the following two hours!

The benefits of exercise are both short and long term. The immediate mood boost, the pride in what you've done, the healthy feeling, the smarts—all of that comes right away. That's the immediate payoff.

You'll experience the long-term benefits over weeks and months as you look better and feel more energetic. And probably most importantly, your body works better. You add quality years to your life. Did you know that active people enjoy on average 15 more years of mobility than sedentary people? *Choosing* to sit on the couch now will literally earn you years of *having* to sit on the couch later.

Get your billion heartbeats.

Your life is a billion heartbeats long. Studies that Swiss-born chemist Max Kleiber began in the 1930s show that no matter what size the animal, whether it's a reptile, amphibian, bird, fish, or mammal (and that, of course, includes us humans), the average number of heartbeats in a lifespan is about one billion.

An arctic whale's heart beats very slowly, between 10 and 40 beats per minute, and that whale's life expectancy is about 150 years. A little hamster, on the other hand, with a speedy heart that beats 450 times per minute, lives about three years.

Apply that principle to humans, and we should only live about 35 years at 72 beats per minute. And in some places in the world, that holds true. But you can actually increase your lifespan if you rev up that heart rate regularly.

It sounds crazy. You'd think that exercise would just sap your billion beats. If you work out three or four times a week, your exercise will consume about a week's worth of heartbeats this year. But just when you think you're using up your billion beats faster than you want to, you're wrong. The benefits of exercise, including a lower resting heart rate, are going to give you 13 more weeks of life expectancy this year. So for every four years of regular exercise, you can expect to add a year to your life.

Soak up the fun.

Have you ever watched children playing? They just get out and do what's fun. They're not worried about heart rate or calorie burn. They just play, and then come back exhausted, covered in dirt, and completely content.

Find a physical activity that's fun for you, and physical fitness will follow. For some people it's seeing what they can achieve in martial arts. Others love running. Others are always on their bikes. For me, it's not so much what I do to work out as how I do it. As long as I work out to music, I find myself caught up in the music video-ness of it all, and I have a great time.

Whether I'm running, biking, or whatever, I like to imagine I'm in the middle of some kind of music video, and everything going on around me goes perfectly to the beat. Sometimes I'm so into it that I'll catch myself doing a white man's overbite with some head groove, and I'll think, *Holy so-you-think-you-can-dance! I hope nobody saw that.* What I'm saying is, do it your way, whatever your way is, and have fun doing it.

My friend Brittney has done a great job teaching her children from an early age that there's fun in physical activity. She and her husband love the outdoors: hiking, biking, golf, fishing, anything outside, and they make sure their kids get out with them. "If my kids know what their bodies can do for them," Brit says, "they won't worry so much what their bodies look like or how they compare to the standard the rest of the world sets."

Play. Have fun. Health will follow, and self-confidence will increase.

Take a deep breath.

Have you ever been stressed out and had a friend tell you to "just breathe?" You've probably even given that same advice a time or two. Why do we say that? Because we all inherently know that if we want to live better, we have to learn to breathe better.

You already know how to do it; you did it as a baby. Watch an infant breathe, and you will see a remarkable sight. With each inhale, the baby's belly fills with air like a balloon, the pelvis rocks forward, the legs separate. The chest rises and then falls like a raft on the ocean. This is what many experts call oceanic, full-body breathing. It has a serene wavelike pattern to it, and it's the way we were meant to breathe.

Unfortunately as we grow older, we gradually lose the perfect rhythm that we knew so well at birth. We become afraid of things, we worry about disapproval, punishment, or disappointment. We experience feelings that we don't know how to handle. We feel tense, and as result, we unconsciously begin to tighten down. We learn to "control" ourselves. We let our muscles restrict our breathing.

Bret Lyon, Ph. D., discovered that the less we breathe, the less vulnerable we feel. The older we get, the more we tend to breathe small and shallow, mostly in the chest, with little visible movement. Most of us, without even realizing it, literally stop breathing for short periods 50 to 100 times a day.

Miraculously, by directing your consciousness back to your breathing, you can learn to let go of patterns of worry and tension that hold you back, and you can return to natural, oceanic, full-body breathing. As your breathing gets fuller and deeper, you can feel yourself softening, loosening, getting more spacious inside. Breathing is like resetting your body and mind.

When you learn to control your breathing and slow it down, you actually slow down your heart rate as well because your heart and lungs work together. With each new breath, new oxygen gets pumped throughout your body. Your circulatory system and your respiratory system are in sync.

If you can control your breathing, you can actually control how fast your heart beats. If your heart starts to beat fast, change your breathing, and it will slow down. And why is that a good thing? Because it lets you make the most of your billion beats. It lets you live longer, with less stress.

Spend five minutes each day focusing on your breathing. Watch each breath go in and out. Let your body move like the ocean. I bet you right now, you're trying it out. Go for it. Take a cleansing breath, and see what I'm talking about.

In through the nose, out through the mouth. Your nose does a better job at filtering the air than your mouth does. In addition, the smaller diameter of the sinuses create pressure in the lungs during inhalation, allowing the lungs more time to extract oxygen. Inhale deeply, then exhale slowly and let the toxins flow out. This kind of breathing helps you get rid of waste products while stimulating your parasympathetic nervous system, which helps you relax.

The way you breathe is the way you live. If you breathe deep before you react to a tense situation, you'll be less likely to say or do something you regret. If you take time every day to concentrate on your breathing, you'll have less stress. Your decisions will be more calculated. Everything in life might just go a little better.

Show me your friends, and I'll show you your future.

When I say that what goes in is what comes out, I'm not speaking only of the physical body. I'm talking about the mind. Your habits. Your outlook. What you achieve.

Your associations have a powerful effect on the way your life will be. Look at the five people you hang around the most. You will find that they are about your same body weight, your income level, your spirituality, your sense of adventure, and your activity level.

Look at who your friends are, then ask yourself, "Is this how I want to be?" If they are not the type of friends who lift you up, you don't necessarily need to dump them as friends. Just add more friends who will give you the energy you need to reach farther. Surround yourself with people who live the way you want to live.

My friend Michael Boyd is one of the kindest people I know. He's also a talented executive who, in his limited free time, travels to schools and youth organizations, teaching young men and women how to choose good friends.

If you're a parent, I know I've got your attention. Michael has the most interesting way of teaching this powerful principle. He calls it the Friendship Quadrant, and the basic message is that every friend you have fits into a category: quadrant one, quadrant two, quadrant three, or quadrant four.

Quadrant one friends are the friends that you are really connected to. You share similar interests, you like to do the same activities, you have the same values. It's effortless. It doesn't matter how much you see each other, it never gets old. It's the right fit all the time. That's quadrant one.

Quadrant two friends are a mirror of quadrant one friends except you're not driven to be around them as often. You like doing things with them, you share the same kind of beliefs, you have the same sorts of likes and interests, but you don't mind having a break at times.

Quadrant threes are fun, but they can also be flaky. Often they do not share your same values. You're a friend of convenience, and if there's a better opportunity or a better option, they'll change plans with you to do something else. They'll be the friends who will gossip to you about others. (And you know what they say: He who gossips to you also gossips about you.)

Quadrant four friends are just your associates. You are only friends with them by circumstance; you work with them or you are around them because of some aspect of your current life situation.

So, Michael teaches young men and women to never be alone with a quadrant three. Quadrant three friends can influence you negatively if you are alone with them for a long period of time because they're not necessarily looking out for your best interest. This is where a kid might think, *Well, I'm a good kid. I've got my act together. I can certainly handle the situation.* And they usually can—for a while. But when things start to break down for that person, it's often after spending time alone with a quadrant three friend.

When you take notice of how your friends influence you, ask yourself, "Is this a quadrant one, two, or three?" Seek to spend time with your ones and twos. If it's a quadrant three, don't be alone with them. But you don't need to be annoyed by them either. Just remember where they fit in your Friendship Quadrant and remind yourself, "They're not one of my quadrant ones, so it's OK if they act this way." Then move toward those who are looking out for you and who will nurture you. Stick by your quadrant ones.

Looking at the Friendship Quadrant logically like this provides you (and your kids) a tool to live by. Michael taught my kids the Friendship Quadrant, and we find ourselves using it all the time. Here's what is so awesome. I can ask my kids as they're headed out to meet their friends,

"What are we talking here? Quadrant one, two, or three?" It helps them evaluate and prepare for what they're about to walk into.

There was a time I asked my son that very question, and he said, "It's a three," then he paused and added, "I'll get someone to come with me." Always take a quadrant one or two with you if you're going to be with a quadrant three. That way you have a built-in support system. Two people can handle one.

Michael teaches this life clue in such an excellent way that I recommend you check out his website: friendshipquadrant.com.

WIND IT UP

When it comes to food, friends, and how you spend your leisure time, does everything line up with what you want? Are your activities taking you in the direction you want to go? Here's a little recap of things to think about; check yourself as you check the boxes.

YES NO

☐ ☐ I eat right 80 percent of the time.

☐ ☐ I slow down and stop when I start to feel full.

☐ ☐ I take five minutes every day to watch myself breathe.

☐ ☐ I exercise for 30 minutes doing something I enjoy at least three times a week.

☐ ☐ I spend my social time with friends who share my same values and who stretch me and encourage me to become better.

☐ ☐ I spend 10 minutes a day reading or listening to something that helps me focus on a topic that's important to me.

CHAPTER 6

DO THE RIGHT THING

Years ago on a winter night, my family and I were eating dinner downtown at a great local burger place called Crown Burger. We have four children, and they were young, so eating out was a pretty sophisticated operation, a coordinated effort my wife and I had mastered. First you place everyone's orders. Then you snag the right table with the right number of seats. You make sure you have enough napkins—you need lots of napkins. Fill all the drinks at the self-serve soda fountain. Straws. Fill up those little cups with ketchup or fry sauce. (If you don't have fry sauce in your area, e-mail me and I'll explain it to you.) Then place all the kids in the ideal seating arrangement.

Finally, we were all ready to eat. Just as I was about to dig into my juicy, flame-broiled cheeseburger and fries, I noticed a distinguished-looking man sitting by himself at a table nearby. He was wearing Army fatigues, and his silver hair was nicely combed. He had in front of him a brown paper sack. Curious, I watched him pull out of the sack leaves of lettuce wrapped in paper towels. Then I watched him nibble on the lettuce, one leaf at a time. My heart ached as I realized this man was most likely eating his dinner from a nearby trash can.

My appetite was gone. I became quiet. Soon my family had finished their meal, and we were ready to leave. Then the thought came: *Just leave your meal, Bryan, and don't make a big deal of it. Help clean up everyone's mess, and leave your dinner behind.*

I'll never forget what happened next. As we were outside getting into the car, I watched this humble man through the window. He quietly changed seats and began to eat a real meal.

My point isn't that I did a nice thing. My message is: I had been given a clue. A gift. A prompting. It said, *This meal is not yours. It is his.*

Knowing that the things we possess are not solely for our own enjoyment and benefit—and giving away a portion of what we have on a regular basis—is the real key to happiness.

Look for opportunities to give to others, even if it seems small or insignificant to you. Don't make the mistake of shrugging off a prompting, thinking, *Oh, that's not even a big deal. They wouldn't even notice that.* Obey that instinct, that life clue. It might make a big difference to someone else.

Your gift doesn't have to be a visible talent like playing a sport or performing music to make an impact. We each have an obligation to find our gifts and share them—to find out why we're on this earth, and make it count.

Follow that first voice.

I will always be grateful for Don Ward, a great mentor in my life. He was the best teacher at my high school. He taught advanced placement history and served as the student government advisor. Approximately 94 percent of his history students passed the AP college credit exam every year, a testament to his genuine caring and concern for those he taught.

One of the things Don teaches kids about taking exams is to pay attention to their first instinct. You've been there, taking a multiple-choice test, choosing the answer, then re-thinking it. Over and over Don has seen students choose the correct answer initially, then erase it and choose an incorrect answer. And the interesting thing is, it's usually the most intelligent students who make that mistake. They get too methodical about what they're doing, and they end up overthinking.

I'm sure you can think of a time that you overthought, whether on a test or otherwise. We've all let our logic overpower an instinct or a prompting, especially if our instinct just didn't seem to make sense. Maybe it was inconvenient. Maybe we were in a grouchy mood, or it was the middle of the night. If there's anything about our instincts that logically don't make sense, it's easy to think, *What? Why?*

But there's something sacred about acting on a prompting. Rely on your faith, and listen to your inner voice. When it tells you to move, get up right then. I guarantee, you won't look back and wish you hadn't heeded your instinct. That first voice is almost always right.

Giving feels good.

Dr. Wayne Dyer notes that kindness actually increases the production of serotonin, the substance that makes us feel happy and peaceful, in the brain. Serotonin is synthesized in most antidepressants, and the increased production of it has been proven to actually have a positive effect on our immune systems.

Dyer said, "Research has shown that a simple act of kindness directed toward another improves the functioning of the immune system and stimulates the reproduction of serotonin in both the recipient of the kindness and the person extending the kindness. Even more amazing is that the person observing the act of kindness has similar beneficial results. Imagine this! Kindness extended, received, and observed beneficially impacts the physical health and feelings of everyone involved."

What do you have that can make others' lives better? Giving makes you a happier, more productive member of society. It prepares you for additional opportunities that come your way. You're more likely to succeed when you look out for others.

CLUED IN: MARTIN LUTHER KING, JR.

"Everybody can be great because everybody can serve. You don't have to have a college degree to serve.... You only need a heart full of grace, a soul generated by love, and you can be that servant."

Life offers so many ways to give. You don't have to give money or food or clothing. Often, what others need most is your time. You can listen to someone. You can drop what you're doing and help someone. You can teach something to someone.

Few things are more rewarding than watching someone you care about, someone you've worked and planned with, reach and accomplish things never dreamed possible before you helped. You see a glimpse of what I'm taking about, for example, when you teach a concept to a child and the child grasps it. You see that light come on, or the little one repeats it back to you or applies it in school or in a game. It's gratifying, isn't it?

What you send out, you attract.

Many times, in order to obtain something, we have to be willing to give that very thing away. If you want more time, give of your time. If you need help, start serving others. If you need more money, be generous. Sharing a talent increases that talent.

Does that sound a little crazy? It may feel counterintuitive at first. Your gut impulse may be to wonder how you're going to get more money, for example, by giving some of yours away. But this is directly related to the law of gravity. Giving keeps that thing, whatever it is, on your mind, and it gives you a positive experience with it. That positive experience starts to take over your thoughts, and you begin to attract it. That's how it works. I'm serious. Give, and it will be given to you.

The happiest people are not focused on how they can *get* happiness. They're focused on helping others be happy, and then happiness naturally comes to them. They're not hoarding anything. At the same time, those who are seeking their own happiness through self-indulgence, trying to make sure they're first in line, taking what they can get when they can get it, often find themselves wondering why happiness eludes them.

Have you ever worked with the guy who acts like there's only so much success to go around? He guards information, is sure to claim credit for his projects, and stresses out about collaborating. He's always keyed up. Looking over his shoulder. Worried that someone is going to get an edge and that it won't be him.

What this guy doesn't know is that the more successful he helps those around him become, the more successful he becomes and the better everything runs. And suddenly, he would be part of something bigger and more successful than anything he could create on his own.

Misery doesn't care what you're thinking, as long as you're thinking about yourself. Jesus said, "For whosoever will save his life shall lose it: and whosoever will lose his life for my sake shall find it." It's a bunch of bunk to think the real solution to sadness or hopelessness is to look out for number one. You may enjoy a temporary change in scenery, but it will never last.

If you're focused on your space and your stuff, how are you ever going to see the clues that life leaves? Open the door. Be in a position to see with the right eyes, listen with the right ears, and feel with the right heart.

Once upon a time there was a little boy who was raised in an orphanage. The little boy had always wished that he could fly like a bird. It was very difficult for him to understand why he could not fly. There were birds at the zoo that were much bigger than he, and they could fly.

Why can't I? he wondered. *Is there something wrong with me?*

There was another little boy who was crippled. He had always wished that he could walk and run like other little boys and girls.

Why can't I be like them? he thought.

One day the little orphan boy who had wanted to fly like a bird ran away from the orphanage. He came upon a park where he saw the little boy who could not walk or run playing in the sandbox. He ran over to the little boy and asked him if he had ever wanted to fly like a bird.

"No," said the little boy who could not walk or run. "But I have wondered what it would be like to walk and run like other boys and girls."

"That is very sad," said the little boy who wanted to fly. "Do you think we could be friends?" he asked the little boy in the sandbox.

"Sure," said the second boy.

The two little boys played for hours. They made sandcastles and made funny sounds with their mouths, sounds that made them laugh. Then the little boy's father came with a wheelchair to pick up his son. The little boy who had always wanted to fly ran over to the boy's father and whispered something into his ear.

"That would be OK," said the man.

The little boy who had always wanted to fly like a bird ran over to his new friend and said, "You are my only friend, and I wish that there was something that I could do to make you walk and run like other little boys and girls. But I can't. But there is something that I can do for you."

The little orphan boy turned around and told his new friend to slide up onto his back. He then began to run across the grass. Faster and faster he ran, carrying the little crippled boy on his back. Faster and harder he ran across the park. Harder and harder he made his legs travel. Soon the wind just whistled across the two little boys' faces.

The crippled boy's father began to cry as he watched his beautiful little son flapping his arms up and down in the wind, all the while yelling at the top of his voice,

"I'm flying, Daddy. I'm FLYING!"

When your focus is on what you can give, you will achieve more than you can imagine.

Just because you can, doesn't mean you should.

Doing the right thing changes the way you see the world. It does something to your expectations because you begin to see the world as an honest place. You treat others fairly, and you come to expect to be treated fairly. You see the good in others because you do good. It works. Doing the right thing brings out something wonderful in you and in those around you.

When my 11-year-old son told me he had landed his first lawn-mowing job with our neighbor, I was 100 percent supportive. It was the perfect beginner job because it was kind of a small lawn. To prepare, we went through all the drills of cutting grass. Yard prep. Watching out for sprinkler heads. When to empty the bag.

When the day arrived, he was ready. He did a really good job for his first time. Then he told me how much the neighbor had paid him. "Wow," I said, "that's a lot of money."

"I know," my son said. "I think I should give some of it back."

I told him it was his call, knowing he would probably do something about it. A few days later I followed up with him and asked, "So what did you end up doing about the neighbor that paid you so much?"

"Oh, I went to his house and slid $10 under his front door," he replied.

"Well, did he see you do it?" I asked.

"No."

"Son, how will he know it was you that slid the money under his front door?"

And then it happened. His eyes lit up, and a big smile came across his face. Without words, he was saying, "Isn't it great, Dad? That's the best part—he's not *supposed* to know!"

I realized that being recognized for returning some of the money had nothing to do with his motivation. He just wanted to do the right thing.

What a wonderful lesson he taught me. Doing what is right and fair will always have rewards far greater than any recognition.

I have a personal motto that I tell my children: "Just because you can, doesn't mean you should." What I mean by this is, look at everyone involved. Are you taking an unfair advantage? Are you looking out for each person?

Jon Huntsman, Sr., who brought us Styrofoam egg cartons, is one of the richest self-made men in America. He has a net worth of more than $1 billion.

Back in 1986, Huntsman was selling a portion of his chemical company. He had a buyer, and they agreed on the price of $54 million. Huntsman planned to use the money for expansion, and he was excited about the agreement.

Months passed as the contract and negotiations were drawn up and finalized. In the meantime, the chemical market had boomed. The sale was now worth $225 million. The buyer was aware of this, and he suggested they split the difference at a sale price of $125 million.

"I will not accept that," Huntsman said. I shook your hand at $54 million six months ago, and that's exactly what you're going to pay for this business." The man kept arguing that he should pay more, while Huntsman argued that their handshake *was* the agreement.

He explained that his integrity was on the line, and that it was important for his children, grandchildren, and corporation to see that when you make a deal, it's a deal.

When you treat others right, you express to them that they have value. But here's what also happens. By treating them fairly and by doing the right thing, you do something to yourself as well. You are making yourself more valuable to your family, your community, and the entire planet.

I like to think about the legendary Ted Williams. Arguably the greatest hitter who ever lived, Williams played baseball for 30 years, accumulating a career batting average of .344 and appearances in 18 all-star games. There's even a spectator seat at Boston's Fenway Park that's painted red, commemorating Williams' famous (and astounding) 502-foot homerun hit in 1946. The ball sailed high over the head of the right fielder, beyond the visitors' bullpen, and kept going for some 30 rows up, until it punched a hole in a fan's straw hat.

More than a decade later, near the end of his baseball career, Williams suffered a pinched nerve in his neck. It was the first time his batting average fell below .300 to .254. That season, he hit only 10 home runs. Still, at the end of the season, the Red Sox sent him his usual lucrative contract. "No, thanks," he said. "I only want what I deserve."

Williams cut his own pay by 25 percent. The next year he raised his batting average back above .300. His final at-bat was a home run. Why? Because his head was where it should have been, and his performance matched it. He did the right thing and that freed him up to enjoy the game and produce better results.

I know many people who are focused on winning the deal. They're driven to come out on top. They can't be happy unless they "win." It makes me sad when I see this. Maybe they've just never tried it any other way.

The following verses were reportedly written on the wall of the late Mother Teresa's home for children in Calcutta, India:

Do It Anyway

People are unreasonable, illogical, and self-centered.
Love them anyway.

If you do good, people accuse you of selfish, ulterior motives.
Do good anyway.

If you are successful, you win false and true enemies.
Succeed anyway.

The good you do will be forgotten tomorrow.
Do good anyway.

Honesty and frankness make you vulnerable.
Be honest and frank anyway.

What you spent years building may be destroyed overnight.
Build anyway.

People really need help but may attack you if you help them.
Help people anyway.

Give the world the best you have and you'll get kicked in the teeth.
Give the world the best you have anyway.

WIND IT UP

Now is your chance to put this life clue to the test. Write down three things you will happily give away, to whom, and when. Here are your three categories:

Your time _____

_____

Your resources (money or possessions) _____

_____

Your talent or skill (mentoring someone) _____

_____

Ask for nothing in return, and don't tell anyone what you did. It's your secret. It will also be one of the best things that has happened to you in a long time.

CHAPTER 7

FINDING HIDDEN TREASURES

When my daughter was six years old she asked, "Dad, what do you want for your birthday?"

"Peace on earth," I said.

"I'm gonna have to get you something else," she replied. "I don't have that much money."

My point in sharing this with you is, too often we tone our dreams down to match what we have instead of reaching for what we truly want. We may have to put our dreams on layaway and keep working toward them until they're all ours, but we should never lower our expectations to meet where we are today.

Create wealth.

I recently watched an interview with Jerry Seinfeld, co-creater and star of *Seinfeld,* a top TV sitcom in the 1990s. According to *Forbes* magazine, Seinfeld's 1998 earnings from *Seinfeld* came to $267 million, making him the highest-earning celebrity that year. The interesting thing is that Seinfeld wasn't necessarily working toward producing a hit TV show. "I just wanted to be a comedian," he said. "I didn't care if I was good at it."

Make sure you're doing what you absolutely love. You may become one of those people who say they never worked a day in their lives.

Opportunities to earn money are everywhere. The thing is, they often take time and patience. There's a story of a young merchant from Boston who joined the California gold rush of 1849. He sold all he had with visions of gold nuggets so big he could hardly carry them. He took to the rivers and began to pan for gold.

He worked day after day with no success. All he had was a pile of rocks. He was discouraged, and he was broke. Just as he was about to give up, he met an old prospector who said, "That's quite a pile of rocks you are getting there, my boy."

The young man explained to the prospector that he was giving up panning for gold. There was none to be found, and he was going back home.

Walking over to the pile of rocks, the old prospector said, "Oh, there is gold all right. You just have to know where to find it." He picked two rocks up in his hands and crashed them together. One of the rocks split open, revealing several flecks of gold that sparkled in the sunlight.

Still, the young man was unimpressed. Eyeing the prospector's bulging pouch, he said, "I'm looking for nuggets like what you have, not just tiny flecks."

Then the prospector opened his pouch so that the young man could peer inside. He was amazed to see that there were no large nuggets, but that the pouch was filled with thousands of flecks of gold.

The old prospector said, "Son, it seems to me you are so busy looking for large nuggets that you're missing filling your pouch with these precious flecks of gold. The patient accumulation of these little flecks has brought me great wealth."

If an opportunity sounds too good to be true, it probably is. Earning money takes work. There are no shortcuts. It's a law of the universe. You have to sow the seed, work through the season, then reap. You simply can't plant corn in the morning and expect to have corn on the cob for lunch.

Please don't misunderstand this clue. I am not saying if the odds aren't in your favor you shouldn't try. If that were the case, we wouldn't have electricity or commercial flight or medical technologies that save lives. No underdog would ever win.

Focus on the word *earn*. Work for it, and in time you will earn it.

Warren Buffett is hands-down the best financial investor of our time. In 2008 he was ranked by *Forbes* as the richest person in the world with an estimated net worth of approximately $62 billion. One of Buffett's basic rules is, *If you don't understand a company's product or how it makes money, avoid it.* He calls this staying within your circle of confidence. Look for earning opportunities that accentuate your gifts and talents.

During the late 1990s tech boom, Buffett famously avoided tech companies, confessing that he could not understand what they did. He looked dumb until the bubble burst. Ultimately, when it came full circle, he was proven right.

Here are some of Warren Buffett's rules:

- If it seems too good to be true, it probably is.
- Always look at how much the other guy is making when he is trying to sell you something.
- Nobody ever goes broke who doesn't owe money.
- Only invest in businesses you understand.
- Look for honest, able management.
- Even if a company has had a few bad years, it can still be a good investment.
- Patience pays: buy 'em and hold on to 'em.
- Buy at a reasonable price.
- The ultimate luxury is doing what you love every day.

Buffett advises, "Generally speaking, investing in yourself is the best thing you can do. Anything that improves your own talents. Nobody can take it away from you. They can run up huge deficits, the dollar can become worth far less, you can have all kinds of things happen. But if you've got talent yourself, and you maximize your talent, you've got a terrific asset."

I have come to learn firsthand that this is true. The best bet I can make is on myself. That is the one element I have 100 percent control over.

Scout talent.

The way to maximize your talent is to leverage it. That is one of the life clues to succeeding in anything you're working on. "Give me a lever long enough and a fulcrum on which to place it," said Archimedes, "and I shall move the world."

You can do the work of many if you tap the right resources. Pay attention to who's good at what, and surround yourself with people who are great at doing what you're not great at.

> ### CLUED IN: ROBERT KIYOSAKI
> "The richest people in the world build networks. Everyone else is trained to look for work."

Those who have built wealth have also built their own network of wealth. Bill Gates has his own operating system and thousands of employees who built it with him. Alexander Graham Bell invented the telephone but also built a business that one day became AT&T. Ray Kroc franchised McDonald's. Each of these individuals became wealthy because they built and owned their own network. They looked for folks who wanted to go in the same direction they wanted to go, and they leveraged the talent.

People who have done well in business understand that their particular roles are not the issue. I once heard June Morris, the original owner of Morris Travel that later sold to Southwest Airlines, say, "Nobody does it alone." That was one of the best clues I was ever given about building a business. You don't have to be good at everything; just find people who play at what you work at, give them stewardships, and get out of their way.

Then, when it all comes together, give those you're working with a piece of the profits. That's an important part! Nothing thrilled me more when a partner and I sold our company than writing hefty checks to the key people who had helped us build the business. It was so rewarding!

Whether you're running a real estate office, an insurance agency, or building a network marketing organization, scouting and rewarding talent will bring you success.

Save big.

Jerry Seinfeld does a comedy bit about night guy and morning guy. Night guy stays up late because being tired the next day is morning guy's problem. It's funny because everyone can relate. But is that how we want to be with our money? Leaving morning guy to retire on nothing?

It's a lot easier to save when you realize that you *are* morning guy. You're not depriving yourself; you're paying yourself. How much do you want to have when you're ready to slow down? Put that much away. Invest in you. Think forward.

It's easy now, more than 100 years after the sinking of the *Titanic*, to see that they should have thought forward. Most of us have looked back at that disaster and wondered, incredulously, *Why the heck didn't they have more lifeboats on board?* It's so clear now how foolish and shortsighted that was.

It didn't start out that way. Originally the ship was equipped with the 40 lifeboats it needed. But the *Titanic* was receiving media attention as the unsinkable ship, and people began to believe it. The spotlight rested on the vessel's beauty and its mightiness. Before it set sail, half of *Titanic's* lifeboats were removed to make the decks look more attractive. The desire for image eventually trumped common sense.

The tragedy of the *Titanic* is not just heartbreaking. It's frustrating because it was so obviously avoidable.

The financial dangers in our own lives may not seem so obvious. It's not so easy to stand back and see the whole picture. But we can take an honest look at ourselves and make sure our lifeboats are in place. When it's time to spend, ask, *Am I adorning the decks, or am I using common sense?*

Make interest work for you.

Albert Einstein is credited for having said that compound interest is the eighth wonder of the world, the greatest force in the universe, and that he who understands it, earns it, but he that does not, pays it. Actually, there is no record of Mr. Einstein ever actually saying that, but whoever did say it was spot-on.

Interest never sleeps. It doesn't rest at night, it doesn't take the weekend off, and it knows no holidays. It's always, always accumulating. If you're in debt, that's a scary thing. But if you're saving and investing, it's a very good thing because interest is accruing in your favor.

I have some cool examples of how interest can snowball in your favor. Let's take a look at 22-year-old Jewel. She just graduated from college, has her first job, and she's ready to save. She diligently socks away $300 every month into an account that pays 10 percent interest. She does this for six years.

Her brother, Owen, does the same thing. Kind of. He's not as smart as his sister. He couldn't stand to scrape that much together each month in his twenties, so he starts at age 32. He puts $300 away each month for the next 35 years.

At the end of that time, Jewel has just as much money as Owen does, right around $1.1 million. Her total contribution was $21,600. His was $126,000. Jewel started earlier, put less in, ended earlier, and let interest work for her.

That's the power of compounding interest. One of the earliest mentions of this concept was by Luca de Pacioli, a man who lived around the fourteenth century. He wrote about the rule of 72, one of my favorite principles. He noted that you can, with compounding interest, divide 72 by the percentage rate of interest to obtain the years it will take to double your investment.

You really don't have to be a math geek for this one—it's way simpler than it sounds. Say your interest rate is 10 percent. You divide 72 by 10, and you get 7.2. That's the number of years it will take to double your investment. If it's 6 percent, you take 72 divided by 6, and get 12 years to double your investment.

For example, if you put $1,000 into a mutual fund that pays 10 percent, and you don't touch it, in 7.2 years, you'll have $2,000. In about 7 more years, it's $4,000. Then it's $8,000, then $16,000. Do you see how this is increasing exponentially? You're not just adding $1,000 every time; the amount doubles, then doubles again, then doubles again on its own.

Let that rule of 72 inspire you. Get your money in there, and leave it alone. Let it do its magic.

Pay yourself.

Finance guru Suze Orman suggests putting away what you need for savings (paying yourself), retirement investments, college funds, and insurances before your paycheck even goes into your account. She explains that if your take-home check is less, "you will quickly train yourself to spend at a lower level, just as you used to do when you were making less money."

It's smart to pay yourself by putting money away and letting it grow. Consider this: The treasure galleon called the *Nuestra Senora de Atocha* sank off the coast of Florida in 1622. This great ship had thousands of Spanish dollars on it. These were large silver coins that would eventually become the forerunner of the American silver dollar.

Since the discovery and recovery of the shipwreck and treasure, you can purchase these old rare coins today in collector shops, jewelry stores, or online. They sell for around $250 apiece, depending on the condition of the coin. I'll tell you more about this little coin story in the afterword. But for now, focus on that one coin, a dollar, that's worth $250 after 400 years. That's pretty good growth, right?

Think about this: If you had inherited a bank account the same year the ship sank, and that account had only one single silver Spanish dollar in it, and it earned just 4 percent *compound interest* since the day the ship sank, you would be able to purchase 16,905 of those coins today. Just one silver dollar would have generated $4,226,384!

I know this is hypothetical, and I know that you're not going to live 400 years, but it points out the power of this incredible tip about making your money work for you. Take advantage of compound interest.

I have found that to honest, good people, money *can* buy a little happiness, if you understand that happiness can be tied to having less financial stress and sharing your abundance with others.

CLUED IN: DAVE RAMSEY

"The goal is to not be normal, because normal is broke."

Spend smart.

We definitely live in a spending culture, and in recent decades, that behavior has become more rampant. I'm convinced that the popularity—and availability—of credit cards has played a major role. I've talked to my parents about the days before the "charge-it" phenomenon, and the rule of life was simply if you didn't have the money to buy something, you didn't buy it. You couldn't. There were just no two ways about it.

The old adage *Fix it up, wear it out, make it do, or do without* is sheer wisdom. Make do with what you have. Then, before you spend money on anything, make sure you need it and that you have the money to spend. If you can't afford it—even if it's only $20—and you buy it anyway, you're going to be $20 short on something you need later. You're essentially cheating your future self.

Buyer's remorse happens all the time, but there is just no such thing as "I passed it over" remorse. It's really unheard of to regret not spending money. Honestly, have you ever thought to yourself, "Wow. I had an opportunity to spend some money, and I blew it!"

Saturday Night Live did a piece with Steve Martin some years back called *Don't Buy Stuff You Cannot Afford.* The characters were marveling about so-called "saved" money, wondering where you could get it. They were

Watch the Clip

dumbfounded at the concept that you should not buy anything if you don't have any money. It's a great parody of what we actually see every day. If you haven't seen it, Google it. You'll laugh your head off because in it you'll see yourself—or hopefully your former self.

When the time to spend does come, be calculated about it. Have a plan for what you're going to spend, and know what, when, and where you're going to buy before you start shopping. Then be disciplined enough to keep your head and not be lured in by store décor or a great deal that makes you excited in the moment. When you follow this plan, you will enjoy a buyer's-remorse-free life.

There is never an urgency to spend, no matter what the most skilled salesperson says. (Yes, the same salesperson who shows you something that's just a tad more expensive than what you said was at the top of your price range.) The temptations to spend when you shouldn't and to spend more than you should are everywhere.

The truth is, it will still be there tomorrow. If it's the last one in stock, they'll get another one in. If the sale ends today, there will be another sale somewhere else tomorrow. That's the beauty of free enterprise. Merchants are fighting for your attention, and they'll do what they can to keep you from walking out of their store with your money. You have all the power.

The late Larry H. Miller, entrepreneur and owner of the Utah Jazz, said in his book *Driven,* "Establish what something is worth to you, whether you're buying a hubcap or a large dealership, and then stick with it." Keep your emotions out of it, and keep relying on what you think that item is worth, not what others are telling you it's worth.

Dave Ramsey will tell you that financial stability is 80 percent behavior—it has more to do with discipline than almost anything else. There's a saying that has some truth to it: Live like you're rich, and you'll always be poor. Live like you're poor, and you will always be rich.

WIND IT UP

If you don't control your money, it will control you. Money is a living thing. It can gain momentum, then just as quickly disappear. It even seems to breathe and grow. And it's easy to lose control if you're not paying attention.

Having less money than you need feels like a ball and chain. Being faced with mounting debt that you can't pay back is a crummy feeling. While having enough (or more than enough) money doesn't buy you happiness, it can give you freedom and peace of mind.

If you have a plan, congratulations. If not, take some baby steps here and get one started.

How much of your income will you commit to pay yourself first each month? _____

What expenses will you cancel right now to free up some funds?

_____

What future expense needs to go on layaway until it makes more sense in your life? _____

What would you be excited to get up every morning to do for a living?

_____

Who do you want to partner with? Who has strengths where you have weaknesses? _____

CHAPTER 8

IN THE QUESTIONS

LIE THE ANSWERS

We all take too much of life for granted. We have so many conveniences that we often forget to ask questions. But everything we take for granted was once a question that had to be answered. Do you ever wonder how our society changed from cash and checks to credit and debit? A little history shows us that nearly 100 years ago, American entrepreneurs were toying with an idea that evolved into the convenient and nearly cashless society we live in today.

Back in the 1920s, the Farrington Manufacturing Co. had a small metal card that looked more like a military dog tag than a modern-day credit card. It was used for gasoline, and generally the service stations would keep the cards for the customer. Could this concept be adapted for larger-scale use?

By the mid 1930s, the emerging airline industry had adopted the idea of an air travel card. By 1941, over half of the airline companies were using the "travel now, pay later" system of payment. By 1948, the concept had spread to international circles. The clues chased each other: If it worked for fuel, then it would work for travel. If it worked for travel, then how about for food?

In 1949, Frank McNamara, head of the Hamilton Credit Corporation, went out to dinner with his business partner Ralph Schneider. When it came time to pay, Frank realized he did not have his wallet. His wife had to rescue him. He vowed never to be embarrassed again, and soon the Diners Club card was born.

Over the next few decades, the card idea continued to gain strength and expand to general-purpose cards. Then came the revolving credit line. From gas to travel to dining to everything you can think to buy, one clue after another prompted the evolution of this amazing plastic wonder of our times.

But I'm curious as to what would have happened if someone would have been paying attention in 1887. At that time, Edward Bellamy wrote and published a novel called *Looking Back*. It was one of the top best sellers of the day, right behind General Lew Wallace's masterpiece, *Ben Hur*. Bellamy's book took place in the future—the year 2000 to be exact. In his story, he described a semi-utopian future world where there was no crime, no politics, and general food storehouses. Eleven times in his novel, he makes reference to the exact term "credit cards," which are used for food or cash.

Business clues are everywhere, but you have to be tuned in. Ask the questions. Be open to the answers. The world begins to change when people ask questions and look for answers.

Every teacher was first a student.

If you assume you know everything, it's difficult to learn anything. Asking questions is essential, even when you're already an expert in your field. Areas of expertise evolve; some completely change every decade or so. Technology is an obvious example, but it's true in every profession.

I've already mentioned that great mentor of mine, Don Ward. While I could write an entire book about all that I've learned from him, I'll keep it brief here and just pass along one more life clue he shared with me.

Every summer for the 35 years that Don taught high school history, he would go to two, three, sometimes even four conferences. By the time he retired, he had attended 106 weeklong conferences—the equivalent of more than two years of his life—studying various aspects of history.

While that, in and of itself, is impressive, here's one of the reasons why he did it: Even history changes! Not just because we discover new information, but also because we judge past history based upon what is going on in our present-day society. For instance, history was unfavorable to the abolitionists prior to the 1950s and '60s. Then came the Civil Rights movement, and all of a sudden, these same people became national heroes. What they had done didn't change, but because we view society differently, our interpretation did.

Don knew that to be an effective teacher, he had to be an effective student. If we are always eager to learn new information—if we're always students—we'll always be broadening our point of view.

Don't fake it.

Believing you know, or acting like you do, can cost you. My seven-year-old son once said to me, "Dad, I have decided not to pretend to speak Chinese anymore."

"OK," I said. "Why?"

"Because I don't want to accidentally say a bad word."

Be willing to do your homework. Look it up. Find out. If you don't understand something, ask. It won't hurt your pride, and you'll be better for simply saying, "Tell me what you mean by that."

This is true in school (it does you no good to pretend you know when test day comes), at work (no one wants to pay you to guess), and in relationships (finding out where the other person is coming from before reacting prevents a lot of miscommunication).

Conversation connects people. Taking the time to find out what others mean and how they feel tells them you care about what they're saying. You'll receive an emotional response that you can't elicit any other way. Conversation strengthens relationships and builds trust. Plus you learn something.

I often work with an experienced filmmaker and audiovisual guru Mark Poulos. He's better than most at what he does, yet he remains humble. If he doesn't understand what someone is saying, he'll stop and ask what they mean. When he and I work together, he takes the time to repeat back to me his understanding of what I said.

Here's the effect his efforts have on our relationship: I feel validated when I'm with Mark, like everything I say is important. I would trust that man with my bank account number. He is who he is—no façade, no pride.

Ask yourself questions.

Asking questions does more good than you may anticipate. You can use this tactic on yourself too. For example, when things aren't going as planned, ask yourself, "What can I learn?"

If you're in a traffic jam, look around you. While you experience that untimely delay, what do you see? What do you have the opportunity to think about? Or if you didn't get a job you really wanted, ask what lessons lie on the periphery of that disappointing situation.

This applies to any situation you find yourself in. Maybe you're dealing with an illness or an injury. Maybe it's a financial setback or trouble with a personal relationship. There's always something in life that we don't think ought to be happening.

Our lives sometimes slow down on purpose. When that happens, refuse to be frustrated. Instead, be fascinated. Hard experiences give us perspectives and empathy we can get in no other way. They open up opportunities to tap into abilities that we wouldn't have otherwise developed.

The questions we ask ourselves when things are hard determine how those hard things will change us.

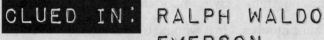

CLUED IN: RALPH WALDO EMERSON

"The years teach much which the days never knew."

One day after a business meeting, I hopped into my car to head to my next appointment. The phone rang. It was my wife. She told me that our 16-year-old son had just been in a car accident. I quickly asked, "Is he OK?"

She said yes.

"Was anyone hurt?" I asked next.

She said no.

After a sigh of relief, I asked what most any insurance premium-paying father would ask: "How bad is it?" She said he had hit the curb so hard that the rear wheel came completely off.

Well, I'm no Sherlock Holmes, but after some questioning and realizing no other cars were involved, it wasn't difficult to see that some poor judgment had taken place. I told my wife I would be right there.

Within about five seconds of hanging up the phone, I was rehearsing the speech I would give my son on Not Taking Things for Granted and the other good one titled A Car Is Not a Toy. And, yes, I wanted to end with the one my dad did especially well. It's called, What the Crap Were You Thinking? You WEREN'T Thinking, Were You?

I got more revved up with every mile I drove. Then it happened, a small modern-day miracle. Over the cell service in my car (hands-free, of course—after all, I was driving under the influence of mild rage) came the voice of a friend hundreds of miles away. She simply said, "Before you say anything to your son, ask yourself this question: If he were a client, how would you treat him?"

What the heck was she talking about? This was no client! It was my son. My son. So much more important than even the most important client. Then it started to sink in. How should I really deal with this? Should it be with disdain and disappointment or with understanding and compassion?

I realized that I could be frustrated without being degrading or unkind. I've done it hundreds of times before. After all, I know this boy. He's the same child who, at four years of age, asked, "Dad, do you know what 'I forgive you' means?"

I told him I thought it meant you're not mad anymore. I'll never forget his eternal wisdom at such a young age. He said, "No; it means I love you."

When I arrived on the scene, he and his mother were waiting. He was probably waiting to hear some form of reproach. His mother was most likely waiting to mend the guilt that I would cause. Except it didn't go down like that. I'm not sure exactly what I said, but I smiled, looked into his eyes, hugged him, and let him know that I loved him.

I wish I could say that had been my plan all along. But it doesn't matter. What matters is someone gave me a clue about respect, and it was enough to make me quit focusing on what my teenager was thinking and instead ask myself what I was thinking. Thank goodness that is what happened. It was my turn to apply what that young man had taught me years earlier: *I forgive you* and *I love you* mean the same thing. I would have missed that if I had spoken before I had asked myself what I was thinking.

WIND IT UP

Here are a few questions you can ask yourself. I believe they will lead you to answers:

What have I been putting off learning? What skill have I always wanted to develop but haven't put in the time? _____

_____

What book will I buy this week?_____

_____

What audio will I start listening to on the way to work?_____

_____

What trade magazine or blog will I subscribe to this week?_____

_____

Who will I call and schedule a lunch with to ask questions about how they do what they do or how they did what they did?_____

_____

CHAPTER 9

GET A CLUE

A few years ago I was playing catch outside with my youngest son. The sun was shining, the temperature was perfect, and a slight breeze rustled the air. It was quiet, almost like nothing else was going on in the world. Unexpectedly, my son stopped and held the ball.

"Son, what's wrong?" I asked.

"Dad, is this a dream?" he replied.

It wasn't a dream, but for him, life couldn't have been any better. It felt like a dream come true.

This experience taught me that whatever you imagine can happen—just as you imagine it can! It might even feel like déjà vu, that eerie feeling that the situation you're in has happened before.

And maybe it has. When you have a déjà vu moment, it could mean that something you want or something you've worked for is happening. You're where you should be.

Emile Boirac, a nineteenth-century French philosopher and university president, was the first to use the words *déjà vu,* meaning *already seen,* to describe that experience. The phrase didn't catch on until a few decades later, when F.L. Arnaud used it officially in a science review in 1896.

It was an instant hit with readers, but why? Because every person relates to this unusual phenomenon. We've all stopped and said, "Whoa, that was weird," and we don't know if it's a repeat of the past or if we dreamed it, but it's extremely familiar.

No one really understands how déjà vu happens, and science has virtually exhausted itself trying to recreate experiences in a laboratory situation. But most agree that déjà vu is an echo of the past, not the future. Something we learned consciously or subconsciously is triggered and, having remained filed and waiting for some release, shoots into your present mental place with clarity. It seems to be different than a memory triggered by the smell of a perfume, a flavor, or a song that instantly takes you back in time. Déjà vu instead comes out of nowhere and surrounds you with the awareness that says, "I have been here before!"

If you leave yourself clues that point you in the direction you want to go, if you set up the right kind of reminders in your life, and if you have enough gravity working for you (see Chapter 1), your objective becomes so familiar that you're able to act more quickly and in a more inspired way. You're able to pick up on subtle clues—opportunities and messages you might not otherwise have noticed. Your actions become automatic, natural—you're in the zone. Then, when things you've planned start to come together, it can feel like a déjà vu moment. You feel like you've been there before because, in fact, you have. You were there in your conscious mind, when you made the choice to work hard, get up earlier, and do the right thing. So that moment of fruition is familiar to you because you've had such a clear vision of it in your mind.

Work on yourself. Get yourself where you want to be *in your mind* so that when you're there *in body*, you'll be able to handle your success. The late modern business philosopher Jim Rohn said, "Best you become a millionaire *before* you get the money, then you will get to keep the money!"

Remember what you want.

We all have to remind ourselves what we're going after, whatever that may be. I keep a family picture displayed in my office. I need to be reminded of what I really want. Everybody needs that in some fashion.

My oldest daughter and I have a text we like to send each other on occasion. It's a simple yet profound question: *R U Ready?* This question has many meanings for us, but the gist is that we are reminding each other to check where we are on the path. When I get that text from her (and sometimes we go months in between) I look at all aspects of my life. Sometimes I text back, "Yes!" And sometimes I have to text back that I need to work on some things. But I love having that reminder to self-evaluate.

Discipline is nothing more than being good at remembering what you truly want so that when distractions and challenges arise, you don't lose your focus—or your determination! Find ways to help yourself remember what you want most, and never trade that for what you want now.

Aron Ralston, the outdoorsman who is now world famous for cutting off his own arm to free himself from a fallen boulder that had trapped him, is the perfect example of finding the grit to do something nearly impossible for the long-term benefit. Most of us can't imagine doing anything like that. But he did, and a major contributor to his triumph was his ability to focus on his future. He made what he saw in his mind become bigger than the dreadful task in front of him.

Ralston's life-threatening accident happened in the spring of 2003 while he was hiking alone in southern Utah. An 800-pound boulder fell and crushed his hand against the wall of a remote slot canyon, pinning him in the narrow crevasse. He knew his situation was grave. Not only was he injured and stuck, he hadn't told anyone where he was going, and his location was secluded enough that he was unlikely to be found.

"The sound of my voice just dissolving into the emptiness in the canyon was so frightening to me," he said. "I took myself to the edge of terror by shouting.... I told myself, *You can't scream for help anymore. You have to keep it together. Don't lose it.*

Five days into rationing his water and trying to free himself, Ralston knew he had a difficult choice: He could either give up and die or amputate his arm. "It was a conversation I had out loud with myself: *You're gonna have to cut your arm off, Aron.* 'I don't want to cut my arm off.' *Dude, you're gonna have to cut your arm off.* I said that to myself out loud in the canyon."

Ralston had videotaped messages to his family and carved his name in the rock with his estimated death date. Then he had a vision of a little boy, a future son, running toward him. He scooped the child up with his arm. That was his reminder. He had to survive.

Watch the Clip

Ralston then broke both bones in his forearm and used a dull utility knife to sever the surrounding flesh and free himself. Try to imagine what that was like. Terrifying. Exhausting. Excruciatingly painful. That's not what Aron Ralston focused on. He said he felt exhilarated in that moment because he knew he wasn't going to die in that place. He then faced a six-hour hike out of that canyon, including a 65-foot sheer wall that he had to rappel, before he was rescued. By that time, he had lost roughly a quarter of his blood volume. But he made it.

This story continually amazes people all over the world. How was he able to do such a thing?

He gives us a couple of life clues. One, he talked to himself *out loud* with firm, decided words, until he found courage (see Chapter 2). Two, he had a reminder—his future—that kept him focused. Incidentally, Aron and his wife Jessica do now have a son.

Take opportunities to talk to yourself. Remind yourself out loud what you want. Talk through what you're doing. Have an inner dialogue. Let your inner self speak because it knows truth. It's been in existence for however long you've been alive. Let your real self come out and talk to you.

Put reminders where you can see them.

One of my best clues on setting reminders came from a strategy coach named Tony Jeary. I flew to Texas once to meet with him for a day. It was awesome. One of the things I learned from him, though, wasn't something he told me. It was something I saw when I went into his office. Off to the side was a workout room, and in that workout room he had a large bulletin board. On it were writings and pictures of things that his kids and family were working on. To me, it was the real reason I was there. What I learned was, if I post reminders of my goals and my family's goals in a location that I can clearly see every day, we will all be more successful.

So now I have that in my office. My corkboard has a schedule of my children's events, my vision, my community responsibilities. I already know what my children's goals are, but these are my reminders. The difference I've noticed in my life is that these reminders make things move a lot quicker. They've increased my interaction with my children, and they keep me focused on my own goals. It's been a powerful planning tool because the important things make it into my schedule because I'm looking at them. They're at the top of my mind, and nothing else is going to fill that space.

If you don't have your reminders where you can see them, your spare time will be filled with things that don't matter. Give yourself reminders. Remember the things that matter, and go after them.

When we make mistakes of any kind, whether it has to do with finances, relationships, lifestyle—whatever—it's because we simply forgot what we really want. We all need reminders, and we can find them all around us.

To really learn from your experiences, write down what you see. If you don't, you'll forget. If you forget, you'll repeat mistakes.

Even little kids know this, whether they realize it or not. They surround themselves with the toys they love. A little boy will carry his favorite car or a pile of rocks in his pocket all day long. Children will role play and pretend to be what they want to be. Some kids won't break character for hours on end. They'll be a puppy or a princess all day.

Older kids do this in a modified way. They put reminders in their lockers at school, they doodle on their notebooks, and they paste things on the walls of their bedrooms. If you want to know where your kids are headed, look in those places. What are they reminding themselves to become? How are they reminding themselves to act? What's pulling them? No kid achieves anything who didn't have everyday reminders of how to get there.

You can do the same. Carry a notepad with you, or download a note-taking app. Jot down clues that will make your life better. Write down things you see others do that inspire or impress you, even if it's something small.

When your mind is clear, you're most likely to recognize and understand little bits of inspiration that will help you in your life. Sometimes you will think of clues while you're falling asleep at night or as you're opening your eyes in the morning. Sometimes clues come while you're praying. Slow down enough to listen. Write down your thoughts the moment they come.

Beware of blind spots.

Failure to see something that is right in front of you does not necessarily mean that you're absentminded or inconsiderate. In life, we are often blinded by stress, entanglements, and challenges that occupy our thinking so aggressively that we fail to see obvious clues. This is a natural thing, not a weakness, and if you know it happens, you can watch it and check it. Here is an example of what I am talking about.

July 4, 1952, was an unseasonably cold morning in southern California. Florence Chadwick jumped into the choppy water of Catalina Island and began the long 26-mile swim to the California coast. Chadwick, the first woman to swim the English Channel, was now attempting at age 34 to become the first woman to make the Catalina swim.

For nearly 16 hours, she fought the cold, the current, and exhaustion while those in her support boats shot at the sharks that continually threatened her. Ahead of her was only a forbidding fog bank. Exhausted and discouraged, she at length insisted that she be pulled into a boat. This was the first time she had ever quit, and she afterward realized that she had surrendered only a half-mile from the crowd that had gathered on the shore to celebrate her victory.

Chadwick later told reporters that if she had been able to see land, she would have made it. The fog had hidden her goal from view, so she gave up.

But not for good.

Two months later, under essentially the same conditions, Chadwick made another cross-channel attempt. But this time she had a clear mental picture of her goal. She held to the image of the opposite shore. She made it, besting the men's record by two hours!

The things we want in life are often hidden in the blind spots of our busy or stressful schedules. We all face times when we must jump into cold, choppy water and swim for a distant goal we might not be able to see clearly. Hold fast to that goal, even when the fog rolls in and the sharks circle.

Now, just a note on how some of us create our own blind spots. It happens when we focus on blame, anger, regret, or other negative thoughts and emotions. Let me share with you what that can do. It will waste your time and your energy, make you less able to enjoy life, and cause you to miss opportunities.

In order to stay upset about something, you have to consciously focus on that thing. It occupies your thoughts, taking up space and pulling you in a negative direction, and you miss out on things you may have otherwise enjoyed. You must expend the energy to look back so you can remember. Otherwise, you might forget!

Looking back means you will most likely miss the wonderful clues that are right in front of you. Besides, if you're hanging onto a negative experience from the past, you might as well still be living it. Let it go! You don't have to—and shouldn't want to—live it anymore.

CLUED IN: DON WARD

"You can either become bitter or better. There's only one letter difference in the words, but that single letter makes all the difference in your life."

Take a life clue from little children. When they get hurt, they stop crying as soon as the pain subsides. They don't want to waste their time on feeling bad any longer than they need to. They want to get back out and play and enjoy the day. A kid who falls off his bike will usually decide not to cry for long because he needs to catch up with the other kids who are having fun. Hurt doesn't drag him down.

And if he decides to "milk" it? Maybe he'd rather have sympathy than fun. Look at what he misses if he stays in Mama's lap. Sure, he's getting attention, but the fun times just pedaled around the corner. They're headed down the block, leaving him behind.

If something is bothering you, let it go. Don't allow yourself to dwell on it. Forgive, and free yourself. It's so liberating when you're not weighed down with a grudge that keeps you from seeing the good things around you. Let the real you get back out and play. The world needs you. You need you. Enjoy the good things that are happening now.

WIND IT UP

If you can't see something, it's hard to focus on it. We all have blind spots. I'm not just talking about the visceral things we refuse to see or the details of life that we miss; our eyes actually have blind spots.

Try this. Pick out a spot on a wall any distance away. Then close or cover one eye and focus on the spot with the other eye. Raise your thumb up, hold it at arm's length, and cover the spot. While keeping your eye focused on that spot, slowly begin moving your thumb to the side. You'll still be able to see both the spot and your thumb as you move your thumb away. Once you move your thumb about 15 to 20 degrees away, it disappears. That is your blind spot!

But here's what's great. Your mind is equipped to handle these blind spots. Take a pen by the tip, and hold it out at arm's length. Shake it back and forth as quickly as you can like you would a fan. It looks like a blur. No matter how hard you try to see the pen in focus, your eyes cannot do it.

Hold the pen again, but this time, hold it perfectly still. Now move your head back and forth as quickly as you can while focusing on the pen. It is not a blur. No matter how fast you shake your head back and forth, the pen stays in focus. Your brain tells your eyes to move the opposite direction to compensate and remain fixated on the pen. (Now, smile at the people who are watching you and wondering what in the world you're doing.)

By establishing reminders for ourselves, we may act the same as our bodies do to counter the blind spots in our vision. When you find a work-around to your blind spots, you can get to where you want to be.

CHAPTER 10

WHAT'S NEXT?

Have you ever been on a road trip that you were totally excited about? You had looked forward to it and planned it in great detail. You climbed into the car with your traveling companions. You took in the energy and thrived on the excitement and anticipation.

But the trip back is never quite as fun, is it? The drive seems to take longer. That's because all you had been looking forward to, you've already done.

It's always exciting when you are on your way somewhere. Having a plan keeps you focused. It keeps you energized about what's next. It challenges you and makes you accountable. If you're not working toward a vision of what you want, you will go stagnant.

Find what's next.

Having a "next" applies to money, health, relationships—everything you do. French philosopher Teilhard de Chardin said, "We are not human beings having a spiritual experience. We are spiritual beings having a human experience." Knowing what's next keeps that spiritual side of you sharp.

Relationship coach and speaker Matt Townsend observes that we all go from hero to human on a daily basis, sometimes more than once. Your spirit is a hero, but the human side of you forgets that. You make human mistakes. Maybe you criticize someone, tell a lie, or get upset about something trivial. The problem is, you become human so often that you forget that you're a hero. When you remember what your potential is, knowing what's next gets easier.

If you're not sure what your next is, don't let that keep you from taking action. Sometimes life just wants you to move, God wants you to move—and *then* He will help you find the answer. But He won't do anything when you're standing still. Even if you're not clear on every detail of what's next, the answers start to come when you start to act. You will find clues, gather information, maybe even adjust your direction. The point is, you'll find what's next when you get up and get going. It's in the moving that you learn.

Lou Holtz, a legendary college football coach, guided four different programs to the final top-20 rankings and led six different programs to bowl games, including a consensus national championship. He is known for his ability to inspire players. He teaches three things we all need to have:

- Something to love
- Something to believe in
- Something to do

Be on the lookout for these three things in your life. What do you love? What do you believe in? What will you do? If you don't know what you're looking for, you will miss it.

Make sure that part of your plan is to have your next plan—and the one after that—lined up. If you don't, you'll achieve what you're working on, and then stop. And when you stop, you're likely to backslide because as humans, we're alive, so we are always moving in one direction or another. If we're not focused on going forward, backward just happens.

You see this in parents whose last child leaves for college, and they don't know what to do next. It happens to people who work hard at a healthy lifestyle, achieve their goal weight, and then begin to gain weight back.

These people got where they wanted to go, and then, because they stopped at their goal, no longer moving forward, they slipped back. Without a next in sight, people not only lose what they've gained, they often fall backwards even further, battling discouragement and depression.

The opposite is true of those who always have a few nexts in the cue. Take, for example, people who run a 5K or half marathon or any race. Before they even run their current race, they're often already registered for the next one. They have a new goal, a new thing to train for, another reason to stay in shape.

The same concept applies with education. You finished high school or college; now what do you want to learn? Surely you've got a list of books you want to read or skills you want to master. Know what you're after and why. Don't make it so difficult that you won't start. Start with small and manageable tasks. But you've got to start. Small things will lead to bigger things.

Anticipating upcoming events, reporting your goals, and being accountable to others keeps you on course. Often on Sunday nights our family sits down, and we each tell what our big plans are for the week. We might share a goal, or a checklist item that's been nagging at us, or a significant assignment. When we declare our plans in front of others, the chances of accomplishing them go way up because there's a new level of accountability. You can have the same experience with morning and evening prayer, stating your intentions for the day and then giving an accounting when the day is over. An effective reporting system makes a significant difference in your chances of succeeding.

When you say something is a good idea, you have a 10 percent chance of implementing that idea. Your chances go up when you say you'll do it, and up again when you say you'll do it by a specific date, and again when you write down a plan.

Now, here's how to pretty much bullet-proof your goal. Find someone to report to, and you have about a 90 percent chance of getting there. Why? Because when you're that accountable, something in you changes. It's not a maybe anymore; you're committed.

Planning is everything about success. You do not have to be an extraordinary person to plan properly and to succeed. Ordinary people excel every day.

Plan to succeed.

By nature we tend to measure success by fortune. The reality is, success and fortune are two entirely different things. People can fall into fortune and good luck, but no one just falls into success.

Success is a balance of well-planned, fought-for, and won victories that involve many things besides money. Joy, social relationships, knowledge, and education are only a few of those victories.

Warren Buffett was once asked his secret to success. He said this: "If people get to my age and they have the people love them that they want to have love them, they're successful. It doesn't make any difference if they've got a thousand dollars in the bank or a billion dollars in the bank. Success is really doing what you love and doing it well. It's as simple as that. I've never met anyone doing that who doesn't feel like a success. And I've met plenty of people who have not achieved that and whose lives are miserable."

Success will always smile on the man or woman with a plan. Nature gives a good clue on this one. Look at animals that hunt in packs. They're strategic, they use their resources (each other), and they are the most successful. A wolf pack, for example, will work as an organized group and bring down prey twice as often as the lone cheetah, who is successful only one out of twenty attempts.

Insects, even though guided by genetics, plan their lives and nests with amazing precision. Using chemical communication, ants build living bridges over streams. Bees follow elaborate blueprints to build technical, detailed hives. Colonies of termites build cities that rival human achievements in scale and perspective.

Remember this fundamental element, a basic clue to getting what you want: An extraordinary genius *without* a plan will be beaten every time and in every way by an ordinary fool *with* a plan.

And here's a cool thing about planning: It doesn't take a lot of time. It's really not a big deal—honest. Just a little bit of planning saves hassle, heartache, and time. Plan your work. Work your plan.

Expect the road to wind.

Now, a word about working your plan. Things rarely go exactly as you think they will, even when you have the smallest details planned out. But having that plan ensures that you'll end up where you want to be. Sometimes you'll even find yourself in a better place than you thought. I have a personal example.

After my partners and I sold our company, Dream Builders, I stayed on as vice president at the new company, SUCCESS Media, parent company of *SUCCESS* magazine. SUCCESS Media is run by Stuart Johnson, a remarkable individual. He and I worked out the sale of Dream Builders together. I mention him briefly here because he personifies so many of the clues we're exploring in this book.

Stuart always gives more than he expects to receive. He does the right thing. When we made our deal, he made sure it was fair for both of us. He genuinely wanted me to win as much as he wanted to win.

Throughout the entire transaction, there was not a single hitch, not one item that didn't pan out as planned. I never had a reason to second-guess Stuart or think he may have taken advantage of me. It was just the opposite. He was my advocate.

As we continued to work together after the sale, his integrity held. SUCCESS was a great environment. I was working with a larger team of talented individuals at a company 20 times the size of my original company. I was still engaged in branding and messaging. But some of the sizzle had gone out of it for me. It wasn't mine anymore. I needed the challenge of the hunt. I wanted to build.

Then came a unique opportunity. It was what I had planned on for my "next"—a position with an up-and-coming company. The product and business plan were exactly in alignment with some personal goals and parameters I had written down 18 months before. All of my reminders and clues pointed in that direction. This opportunity was what I needed. It allowed me to get back in the hunt again. To create. To do the from-the-ground-up thing and be challenged in a new way.

The deal was months in the making, and all of the concerns and worries that come with making a big career change took over my mind during the decision-making process. It was hard to think of leaving SUCCESS Media. One of the people I dreaded telling was, of course, Stuart.

His calm, kind reaction shouldn't have surprised me. Not one word about his company or himself came out of his mouth. It was all about me. He wanted to be sure that this new venture was right for *me* and that it fit where *I* wanted to go in *my* life. Even though I had I just told him that I was ready to separate, he was still contributing to *me*. By the way, Stuart still checks up on me from time to time.

The first year of my new venture was all I had expected it to be. Then things started to shift. The direction the company was taking was suddenly out of alignment with my vision. My first instinct was to line it all back up, so I focused on that and tried everything I could think of. But I couldn't make it happen. Ultimately, I knew the only thing I had power to change was myself. It would be me who would have to part ways. It was disappointing and disheartening. I even questioned if my initial decision to go with this company had been right.

I can tell you now that it absolutely had been. That move was a stepping stone that had to impersonate *the* opportunity for me, or I wouldn't have stepped on it. And it paved the way for me to start doing full-time the things that are completely in line with all my "nexts." I can say with certainty that I would not be where I am if that opportunity had not come, and if I had not taken it.

Next time an opportunity comes to you, just know that it could look like the next big thing, but it may disappoint. The road may wind in ways you didn't expect. The important thing is, where did it lead you? Winding roads will sometimes show and teach you things that you may not have learned in any other way. It can put you in a better position than you could have created for yourself.

Don't get frustrated when the path you choose turns out to be a strange, unfamiliar, and even difficult one. Sometimes doing what is right and what's next come only after doing some of the hardest things you will ever do. But if you could peer around the corner, you would see yourself arriving exactly where you need to be.

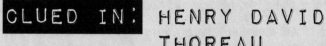

CLUED IN: HENRY DAVID THOREAU

"If one advances confidently in the direction of one's dreams, and endeavors to live the life which one has imagined, one will meet with a success unexpected in common hours."

WIND IT UP

Your nexts don't have to be big, huge goals. Some can be, but you also need little nexts that you can do every day. Finish your day before you start. It's easy if you just use the number seven.

You already have a relationship with that number. Seven digits in your phone number, seven days of the week, seven colors of the rainbow, seven basic musical notes. Oh, and one more thing: seven things to do each day.

Before you go to bed each night, write down the seven things you're going to get done tomorrow. Plan your day before it starts, so when you wake up, you've got those things ready to be accomplished. It will create momentum that will carry you through your day. Those nexts have power!

By the way, here's my personal next: *Life Leaves Clues, Volume 2*. Gravity is pulling, and I can't ignore it. There are so many more clues to share!

Oh, and as you get your clues, shoot them to me in an e-mail at bryan@lifeleavesclues.com. I would love to hear about and share the life clues you have found. People all over the world are waiting to discover them too. I know I am.

And if you like me, tell me. Go to facebook.com/lifeleavesclues, and click the like button. That's where all my *Life Leaves Clues* friends share their ideas and insights. And yes, you'll catch me tweeting now and again.

AFTERWORD

Every person has a different ball of string to wind. Yours isn't like anyone else's. Your clues are uniquely your own. Paying attention to your clues will lead you to your individual potential and bring you the most contentment.

There's a great story—a true story—that illustrates what I'm talking about. As a child, Melvin Fisher was fascinated by Robert Louis Stevenson's *Treasure Island*. From his love of that book, he developed an interest in scuba diving. But like most 11-year-olds, he didn't have much opportunity to learn to dive. Mel hung onto that interest while he lived a normal childhood in Indiana. He went to college and graduated, served in World War II, and eventually settled in California, where he and his family owned a chicken farm.

Mel met his wife, Deo, around that time. Together they worked the farm. But Mel had always kept alive his lifelong interest in breathing and exploring underwater. He learned scuba, and he and Deo eventually opened California's first dive shop. They ran it out of a shed on the chicken farm.

It was the early 1950s, and there was a resurgence of interest in gold; sort of a revisitation of the 1849 Gold Rush that had brought thousands of pioneers to California a century earlier. Tourists and residents alike loved to pan for gold. Melvin was intrigued as well. He had never forgotten *Treasure Island*, he still loved all that was underwater, and now he actually had the freedom and the know-how to explore.

So here's what Mel and Deo did. They started selling dive equipment and hosting adventure trips for people who wanted to explore the ocean for the first time. Their business grew to the point that the shed wasn't big enough anymore. They needed a new building, which they put up literally brick by brick, diving for lobsters to pay for it. The sale of each lobster purchased seven bricks.

Together Mel and Deo fostered their love of diving, and Deo eventually broke the record for staying underwater. The previous record stood at 50 hours, and Deo achieved 55 hours, 37 minutes. Media attention brought publicity and new business. In time, the Fishers made films about diving in exotic places, and Mel's underwater adventures aired on television.

All the while, Mel and Deo treasure hunted. The pursuit eventually led them to team up with other divers who were searching for sunken treasure fleets. This took them to Florida, where they and their partners opened Treasure Salvors. Now they were true treasure hunters. No more diving in creeks in the mountains of California, trying to find a nugget of gold. Now they were searching for lost Spanish fleets reported to have untold fortunes.

They worked what they loved for years, sometimes finding bits of treasure, sometimes coming up empty-handed. Finally, after 16 years, they found the Spanish galleon *Nuestra Senora de Atocha*, which had sunk in a hurricane in 1622.

Reports say that when Melvin's divers found the fortune, he was out shopping in the small community of Key West, Florida. The local radio station was broadcasting, "If anyone has seen (Melvin), tell him he's found the big pile!" As he exited the store, well wishers were waiting to congratulate him on the street.

That was July 20, 1985. The find was worth an estimated $450 million.

Don't get me wrong. I don't want to focus on that $450 million. That's just what happened to Mel Fisher when he followed the clues that life left for him.

Becoming what you should be is about finding your right path, following what you love, learning to work with your life, and doing what's right for you even if others can't see it. I believe that life is your advocate. Life is on your side, like a loyal team member that shows you your ultimate potential.

We live our lives surrounded by clues, and our ability to see them and apply them changes us. We become more each day than what we were the day before as we follow the promptings of life's clues. It is important to realize that you are a part of this great performance of life. You are being watched, admired, and copied. You leave clues for others to recognize and follow.

Through your success, others become capable of achieving more. A kind word at the proper moment, a warm smile, a helping hand when it is unexpected, all can be clues that make someone's day or even change someone's life. Someone watching or listening to you may be moved at the perfect time because of a clue you shared.

Many of these clues you already know but may have forgotten or just not acted on in a while:

Each day, pay a sincere complement to someone you don't know yet.
Each day, hug someone you love.

Each day, write in a diary or a journal.

Each day, question something, research something.

Each day, do a kind act for someone anonymously.

Each day, express what you are grateful for.

Each day, say, "I love you," and mean it.

Each day, pray.

I know that you know these simple truths. You have heard them many times, but ask yourself, *Am I acting on them?*

Begin a new day today. So many gifts of life await you as you start with renewed vigor. Make a conscious effort to find the clues that life is waiting to bestow on all of us who are watching for them. Through your example, you will *leave* your own clues to bless others as they observe and admire you.

GET CLUED IN

Visit BryanThayer.com to for more valuable life clues. And if you really want to clue in, subscribe to his free newsletter and you'll receive a free audio from his best-selling book *The One Minute Networker* at BryanThayer.com/newsletter.

Find and like Bryan on Facebook, follow him on Twitter, and check him out on YouTube!

facebook.com/lifeleavesclues
twitter.com/lifeleavesclues
youtube.com/lifeleavesclues

You can get additional copies of *Life Leaves Clues* and other Bryan Thayer products at BryanThayerStore.com.

Have Bryan speak at your next event!
Need a little inspiration and motivation for your organization? Bryan Thayer will energize your group with his fun and innovative ways of teaching people to achieve greater success. For more information, visit BryanThayer.com/speaker.

NOTES

NOTES

NOTES

NOTES

NOTES